NEW TRENDS IN GUI

SendPoints

NEW TRENDS IN GUI

©2017 SendPoints Publishing Co., Ltd.

SendPoints

EDITED & PUBLISHED BY SendPoints Publishing Co., Ltd.

PUBLISHER: Lin Gengli

PUBLISHING DIRECTOR: Lin Shijian

ASSISTANT PUBLISHING DIRECTOR: Chen Ting

CHIEF EDITOR: Lin Shijian

LEAD EDITOR: Lin Qiumei

EXECUTIVE EDITOR: Akira Ho   Claire Wei

ART EDITOR: Lin Shijian

EXECUTIVE ART EDITOR: Lin Qiumei

PROOFREADING: Marie Valentine

REGISTERED ADDRESS: Room 15A Block 9 Tsui Chuk Garden, Wong Tai Sin, Kowloon, Hong Kong

TEL: +852-35832323 / **FAX:** +852-35832448

OFFICE ADDRESS: 7F, 9th Anning Street, Jinshazhou, Baiyun District, Guangzhou, China

TEL: +86-20-89095121 / **FAX:** +86-20-89095206

BEIJING OFFICE: Room 107, Floor 1, Xiyingfang Alley, Ande Road, Dongcheng District, Beijing, China

TEL: +86-10-84139071 / **FAX:** +86-10-84139071

SHANGHAI OFFICE: Room 307, Building 1, Hong Qiang Creative Zhabei District, Shanghai, China

TEL: +86-21-63523469 / **FAX:** +86-21-63523469

SALES MANAGER: Sissi

TEL: +86-20-81007895

EMAIL: sales@sendpoints.cn

WEBSITE: www.sendpoints.cn / www.spbooks.cn

ISBN   978-988-77573-6-8

With the rapid development of science and technology, what changes have taken place in interactive design? How much do you know about data visualization, the involvement of Augmented Reality/Virtual Reality technologies and the increasing invisibility of interfaces? Whether you are a novice or a senior designer, it is necessary to keep up with the new trends and thus create a better product. Please turn this page and go on reading: a large amount of information and examples are waiting for you!

CONTENTS

FUNCTIONAL INTERACTION DESIGN

SOCIAL
INTERACTION DESIGN

Do you know any social apps besides Facebook and Twitter? This chapter introduces some and illustrates the role that interaction design plays in social media.

INSTANT MESSAGING

 GROUP CHAT

 DATING

 PERSONAL COMMUNITY

INTERACTION DESIGN SHOULD BE USER-CENTERED

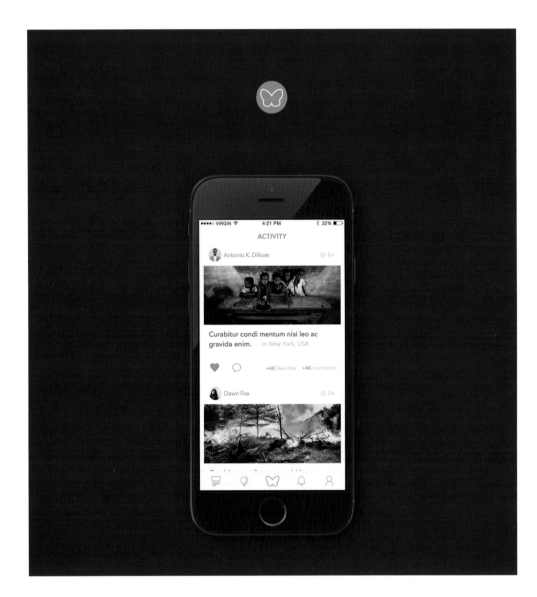

Francisco Junior
Brazil
Visual Designer
UX Designer

Interaction design is embedded in products that are part of our daily life. Its goal is to ease the use of a product, whether it is a tangible product such as an electronic device or an intangible product such as software.

The design of these products is thought to make them effective, enjoyable and easy to understand for those who will handle them.

For this to happen, it is important to have the user in mind when creating a website, an application or a device, etc. The designer should consider the needs of the user, the amount of time that it will be used, and the actions that the user wants to accomplish with it.

In developing this concept, the designer provides new possibilities to the business of their customers and improves the relationship between the product and the user. Therefore, innovative services and products that contribute to the success of a brand will be created.

To realize the interaction design, however, some important aspects should be taken into consideration. First of all, the interaction designer needs to think about how the product fits into the user's life——the usefulness (or futility). Second, the designer needs to assess emotional aspects of the product. An interactive product may have no practical value, but possess tremendous emotional relevance. Besides, a number of other aspects should be considered such as safety, social behavior, politics, semiotics, persuasion, information design and affordability.

When I start designing any product or service, **the search for user knowledge and understanding is crucial.** Being close and understanding their journey, their wishes and desires creates empathy. All of this is critical to providing authentic experiences and engaging a person.

Although each of us has our ways of working, **we are all designing for people. And people are intuitive: they do not like to think.** So when they are forced to do so, it may indicate that what you designed is not suitable for that scenario.

In my work, I always try to create clean interfaces and use lots of white space to help people locate things and get the sense of organization. The use of colors and icons are also essential, since with little explaining you can contextualize situations in visual ways without having to force the user to read or understand.

Besides, I really enjoy playing with typographies, working its weight variations and sizes. **I believe that with well-resolved use of typography, we can give a personality to an interface.**

Interaction design will become a key process in the development of a product, be it a web platform, a mobile application or service/products with voice interface.

CHANGE IT

Designer: Francisco Junior

Change It is a creative mobile app for leaders globally. They can post their ideas for community improvements and take photos of problems or challenges in their communities with a location pin.

 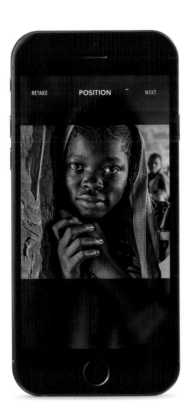 

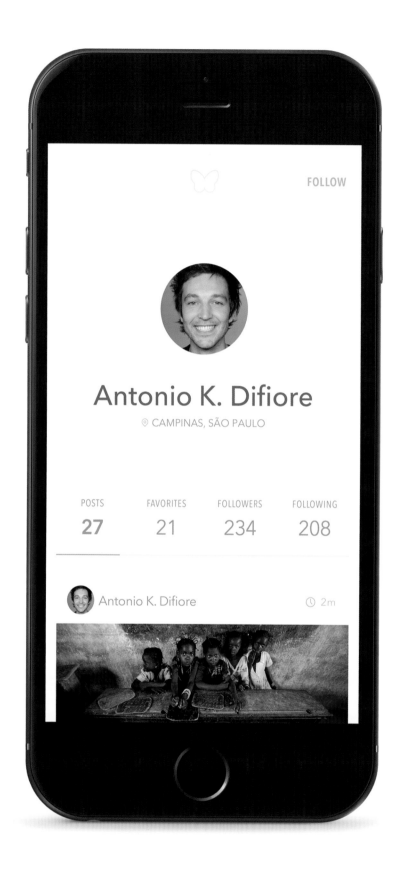

Antonio K. Difiore

⊙ CAMPINAS, SÃO PAULO

POSTS	FAVORITES	FOLLOWERS	FOLLOWING
27	21	234	208

Antonio K. Difiore   🕐 2m

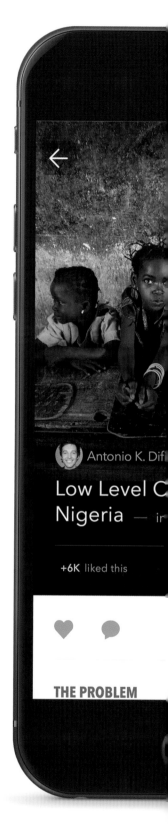

Antonio K. Dif

Low Level C
Nigeria — ir

+6K liked this

THE PROBLEM

SPLISH

Designer: Kristijan Binski   Country: Serbia

Not your average shallow dating app, Splish is a fast-paced mobile dating game that lets you choose matches based on their answers to questions from the Splish question bank. Favorite ice cream? Secret talent? Choose a winner and then message your match with one of the witty icebreakers.

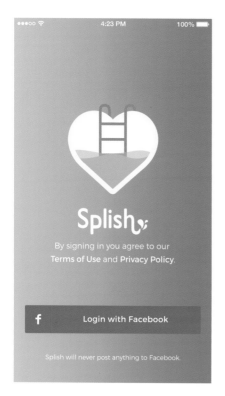

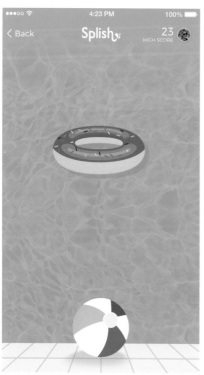

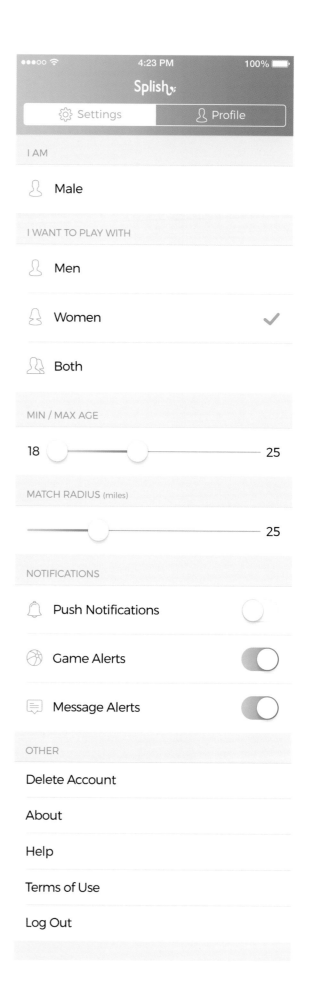

Dating Pool

Game Questions

Chat

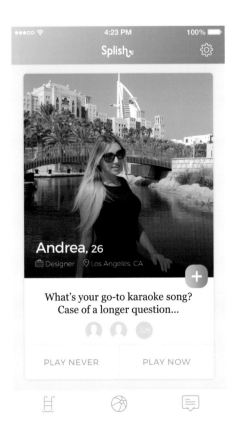

Andrea, 26

🏢 Designer   📍 Los Angeles, CA

What's your go-to karaoke song?
Case of a longer question...

PLAY NEVER   PLAY NOW

Andrea wants to know...

✓ ANSWERED

What's your go-to karaoke song?
Robbie Williams - Feel

✓ ANSWERED

Do you believe in ghosts?
Why or why not?
Example of a slightly longer answer and a
second line of text if needed....

TAP TO ANSWER

What is the last book you read?

SUBMIT

Andrea

Hey!

I really liked all your answers.

Hello Andrea!
6:54 PM

I am happy to hear that! Now
it's my turn to ask a couple of
questions... Hope you don't
mind? 😅
6:54 PM

Type a message...

BEACH LOVE

Designer: Marco Santonocito   Country: Italy

SportFelix is an Italian tour operator focusing its activities in the ideation, promotion and organization of international sports, educational trips, camps and trainings. And Beach Love is an application that can be used during the events, which every year gather more than 20,000 attendees. The goal of this application is allowing people to meet other attendees and ask them to hang out. This will eventually leads to finding their true love.

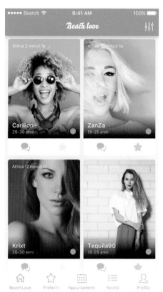

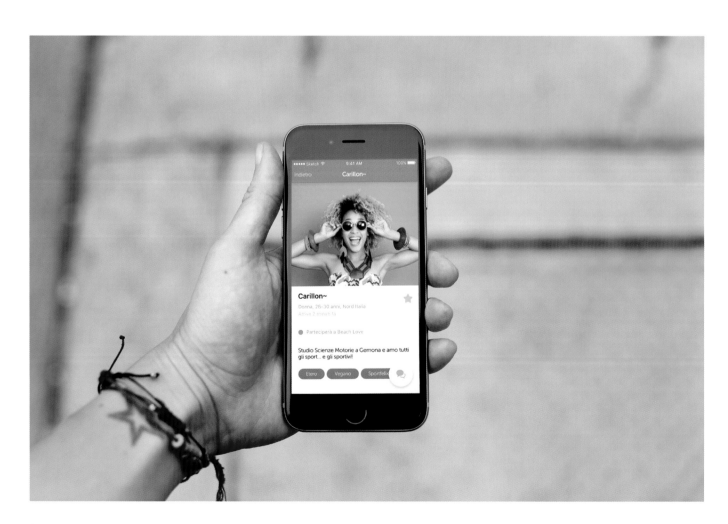

Ricevi o invia richieste
a chi ti piace di più

Scopri di più su BeachLove

Richiesta ricevuta!

Stella92 vuole incontrarti!

● ● ●

Iscriviti ora!

Già 2.348 persone sono su BeachLove.

Incontra chi ti piace e chissà,
magari scatta qualcosa!

Scopri di più su BeachLove

Scatta il limone!

● ● ●

Iscriviti ora!

Già 2.348 persone sono su BeachLove.

Cancella   **Filtri**   Fatto

Filtra la lista dei partecipanti
in base alle tue preferenze!

Sesso   ⌄

Fascia d'età   ⌄

Regione di provenienza   ⌄

Eventi BeachLove

☐ Mizuno Beach Volley Marat...
    19 - 21 Maggio

☐ B5FootballCup
    20 - 21 Maggio

☐ Beach Volley Marathon
    9 - 11 Giugno

☐ Bibione&Beach Fitness
    15 - 17 Settembre

☐ Mizuno Beach Volley Marat...
    15 - 17 Settembre

☐ Foto profilo

☐ Attivo nelle ultime 24h

Caratteristiche

(Etero) (Omo) (Bisex)

(Vegano) (Sportfelix)

(Pirata)

Filtra

UTENTE NON LOGGATO

00. Caricamento

00.00

01. Onboarding

01.00

02. Sign in / Sign up

02.00

02.03

02.01

02.04

02.02

UTENTE LO

03. Utenti

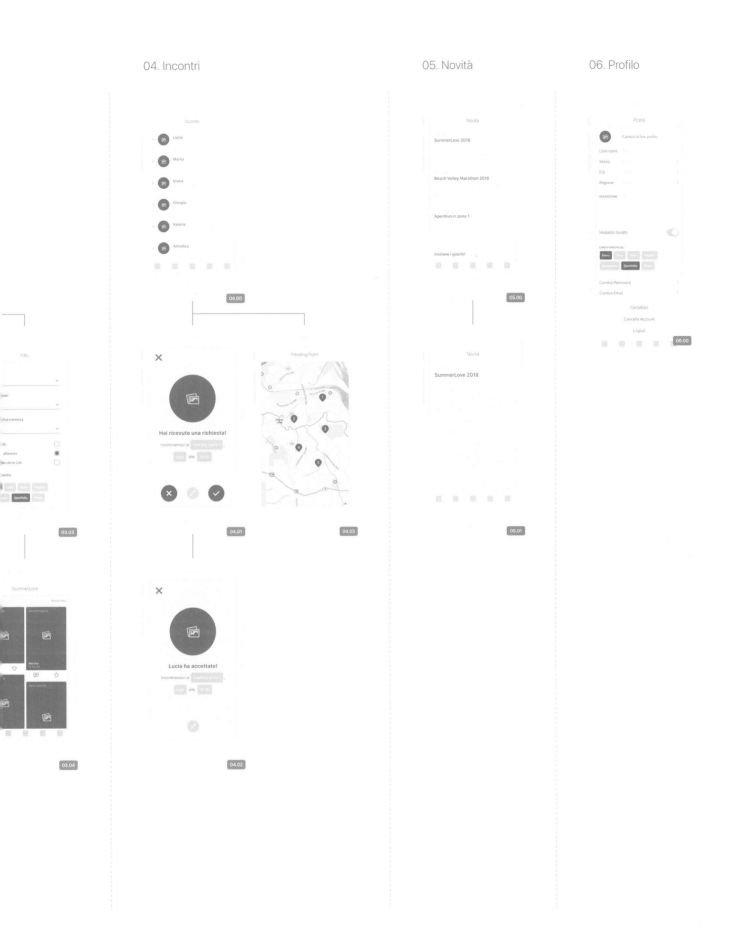

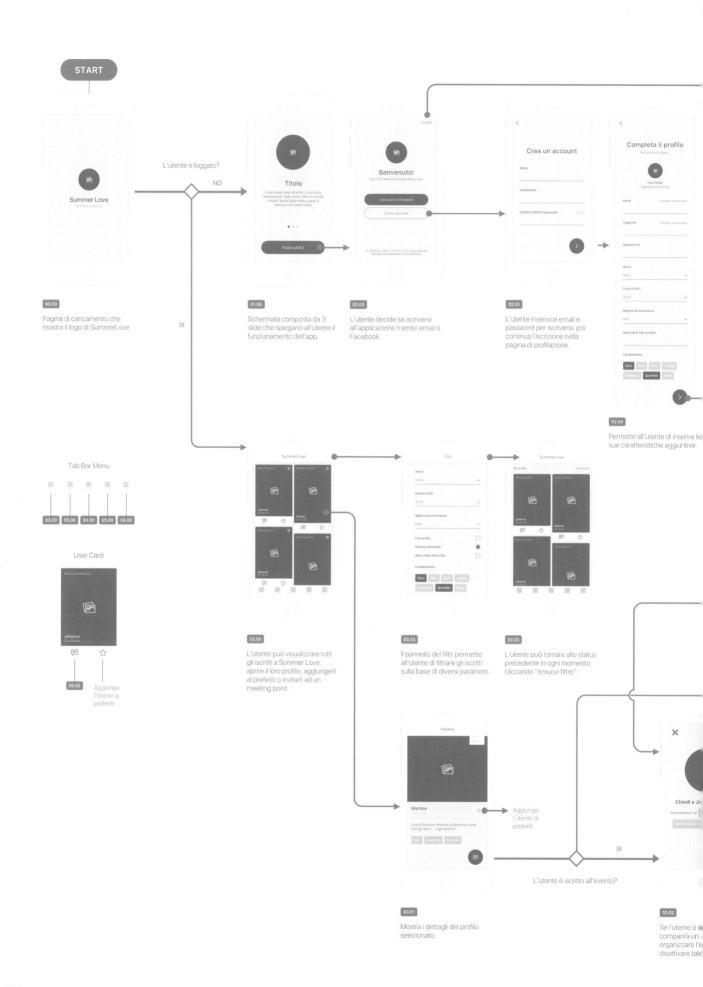

START

00.00

Pagina di caricamento che mostra il logo di SummerLove

L'utente è loggato?

NO

SI

01.00

Schermata composta da 3 slide che spiegano all'utente il funzionamento dell'app.

02.00

L'utente decide se iscriversi all'applicazione tramite email o Facebook.

02.03

L'utente inserisce email e password per iscriversi, poi continua l'iscrizione nella pagina di profilazione.

02.04

Permette all'utente di inserire le sue caratteristiche aggiuntive.

Tab Bar Menu

03.00 03.00 04.00 05.00 06.00

User Card

03.02

Aggiunge l'utente ai preferiti

03.00

L'utente può visualizzare tutti gli iscritti a Summer Love, aprire il loro profilo, aggiungerli ai preferiti o invitarli ad un meeting point.

03.03

Il pannello dei filtri permette all'utente di filtrare gli iscritti sulla base di diversi parametri.

03.03

L'utente può tornare allo status precedente in ogni momento cliccando "rimuovi filtro".

Aggiunge l'utente ai preferiti

L'utente è iscritto all'evento?

SI

03.01

Mostra i dettagli del profilo selezionato,

03.02

Se l'utente è i... comparirà un... organizzare l'i... disattivare tale...

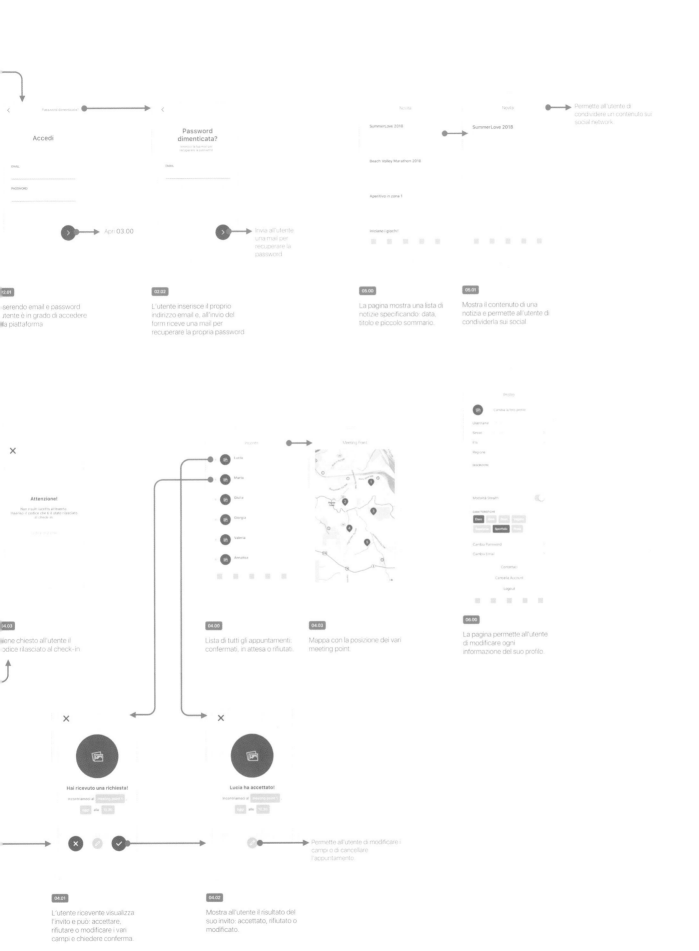

Accedi

Password dimenticata

EMAIL

PASSWORD

Apri 03.00

02.01

Inserendo email e password l'utente è in grado di accedere alla piattaforma

Password dimenticata?

EMAIL

Invia all'utente una mail per recuperare la password

02.02

L'utente inserisce il proprio indirizzo email e, all'invio del form riceve una mail per recuperare la propria password

Novità

SummerLove 2018

Beach Volley Marathon 2018

Aperitivo in zona 1

Iniziano i giochi!

05.00

La pagina mostra una lista di notizie specificando: data, titolo e piccolo sommario.

Novità

SummerLove 2018

Permette all'utente di condividere un contenuto sui social network

05.01

Mostra il contenuto di una notizia e permette all'utente di condividerla sui social

×

Attenzione!

Non risulti iscritto all'evento. Inserisci il codice che ti è stato rilasciato al check-in

04.03

Viene chiesto all'utente il codice rilasciato al check-in

Incontri

Lucia

Marta

Giulia

Giorgia

Valeria

Annalisa

04.00

Lista di tutti gli appuntamenti: confermati, in attesa o rifiutati.

Meeting Point

04.03

Mappa con la posizione dei vari meeting point.

Profilo

Cambia la foto profilo

Username

Sesso

Età

Regione

Descrizione

Modalità Stealth

CARATTERISTICHE

Elena

Sportfolio

Cambia Password

Cambia Email

Contattaci

Cancella Account

Logout

06.00

La pagina permette all'utente di modificare ogni informazione del suo profilo.

×

Hai ricevuto una richiesta!

Incontriamoci al

04.01

L'utente ricevente visualizza l'invito e può: accettare, rifiutare o modificare i vari campi e chiedere conferma.

×

Lucia ha accettato!

Incontriamoci al

Permette all'utente di modificare i campi o di cancellare l'appuntamento.

04.02

Mostra all'utente il risultato del suo invito: accettato, rifiutato o modificato.

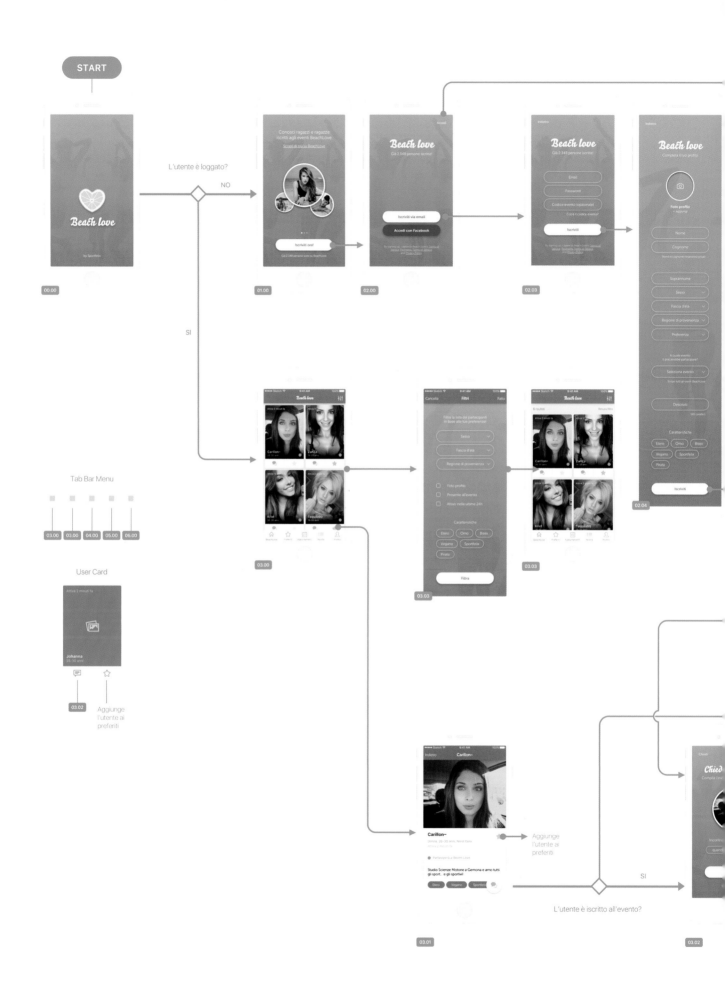

START

L'utente è loggato?

NO

SI

00.00

01.00

02.00

02.03

02.04

Tab Bar Menu

03.00   03.00   04.00   05.00   06.00

User Card

Johanna
25-30 anni

03.02

Aggiunge
l'utente ai
preferiti

03.00

03.03

03.03

03.01

03.02

Carillon~

Aggiunge
l'utente ai
preferiti

L'utente è iscritto all'evento?

SI

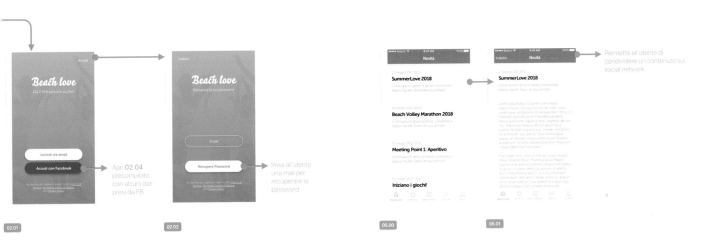

02.01

02.02

05.00

05.01

Permette all'utente di
condividere un contenuto sui
social network.

Apri 02.04
precompilato
con alcuni dati
presi da FB

Invia all'utente
una mail per
recuperare la
password

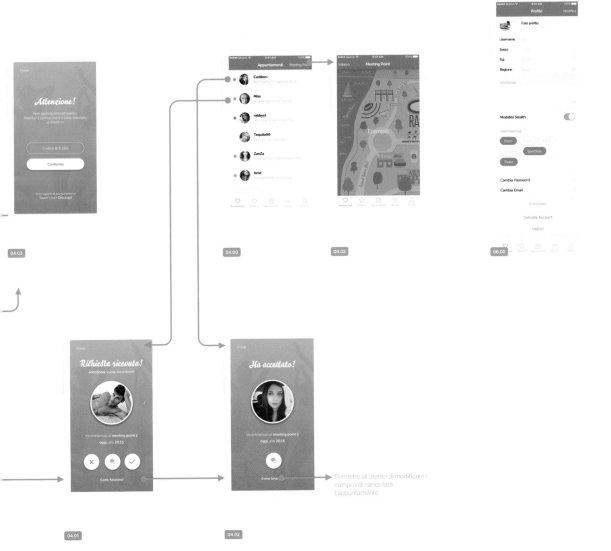

04.03

04.00

04.03

06.00

04.01

04.02

Permette all'utente di modificare i
campi o di cancellare
l'appuntamento

THE LACK OF A VISIBLE UI WILL BECOME THE NEW TREND

Anton Avilov
Russia
UI/UX Designer

Although there are no universal rules in the process of modern interactive design, psychological profiling is an essential part and it significantly differs from case to case. It is critical to define your target audience and project tasks from the start since it is what affects users' behavior. The deeper you understand your users, the better you are as an influencer. Standalone emotions like anger or desire are not responsible for design strategy, while overall psychological profile is always classified and used later for that purpose.

Colors, images and typography are building blocks for interactive designers, while the most important part is how to combine them in a proper way. Combining these elements to craft a unique appearance creates a special feeling and identity associated with the project.

The future of interactive design is based on user interface simplification, making a feeling of intuitive and straightforward usage. **It is perfect when interactive design becomes less visible for the end user, when it seems that he seamlessly interacts with the product in his hands.**

U&ME

Designer: Anton Avilov

U&Me is a simple mobile app for iOS which has functional ability for collaboration and communication.

Sign In

Simple and simple registration with
mobile phone number and
confirmation via SMS

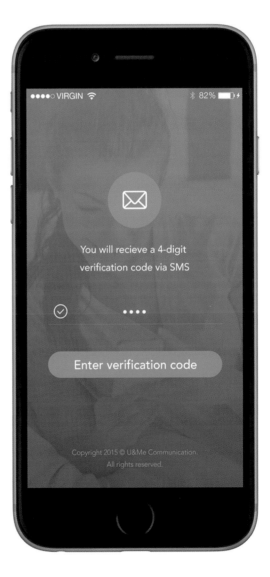

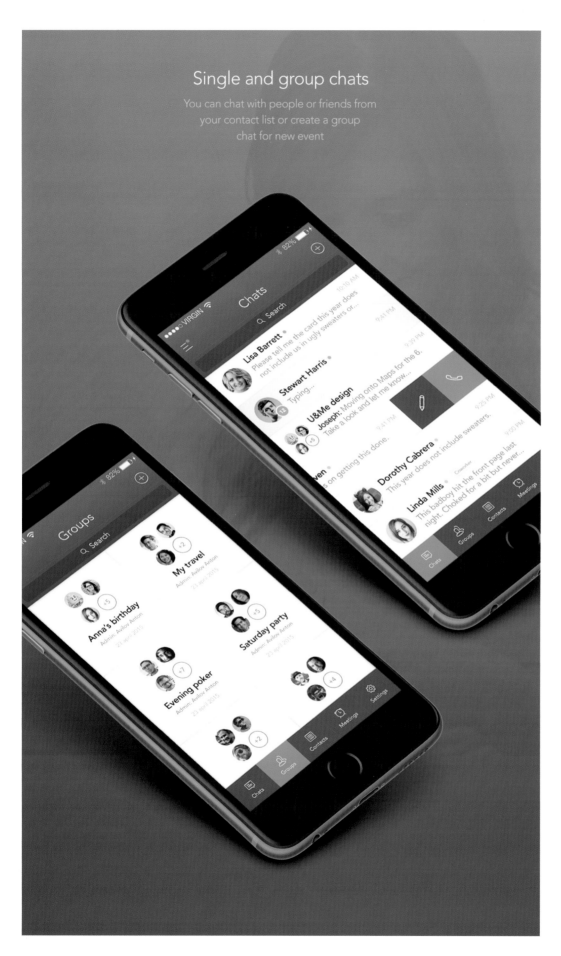

Single and group chats

You can chat with people or friends from
your contact list or create a group
chat for new event

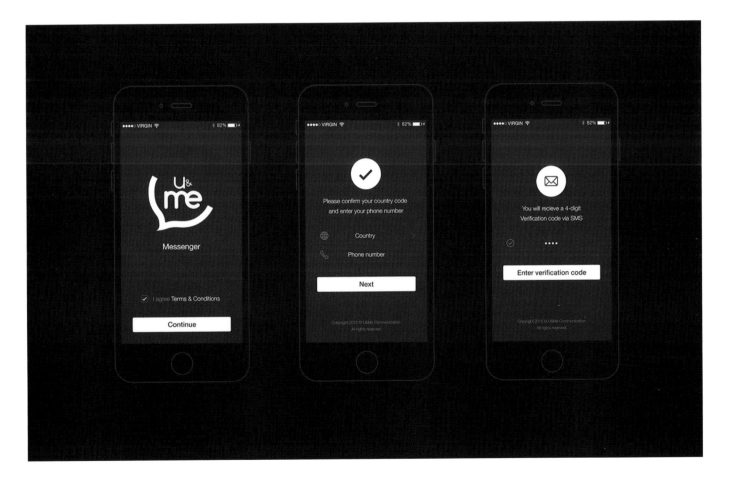

Ska Vi Ses is an online dating app for shy young people. It does not have chat options. People can send pokes to each other instead. When pokes are mutual, the app allows users to make a call or send a date invitation. The colorful interface is intuitive and eye-catching for teenagers.

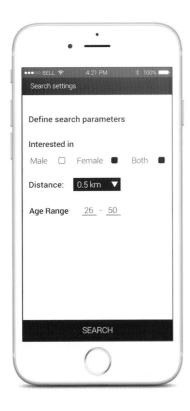

Search settings

Define search parameters

Interested in

Male ☐   Female ■   Both ■

Distance: 0.5 km ▼

Age Range   26 - 50

SEARCH

Registration

Alias

First Name

Last Name

e-mail

Select Date of Birth 📅

Choose your gender

Matches

Jhon Doe
17.06.1953   17.06.2015

Jhon Doe
17.06.1953   17.06.2015

Jhon Doe
17.06.1953   17.06.2015

Jhon Doe
17.06.1953   17.06.2015

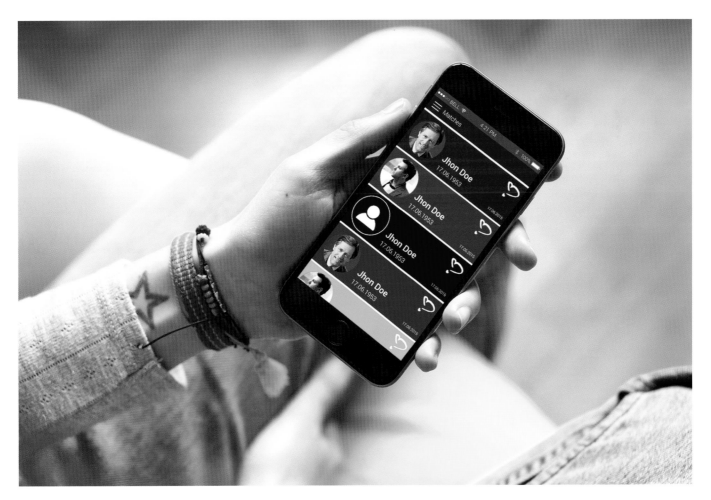

Alias

First Name

Last Name

e-mail

Select Date of Birth 📅

Choose your gender

Male ⬜ Female ⬛

Interested in

Male ⬜ Female ⬛ Both ⬛

Age Range 26 - 50

CONTINUE

Registration screen step 1

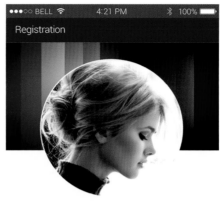

Add more photos and video

* You can add 2 more photos that will be shown to your matches.

* Video can't be longer than 10 seconds.

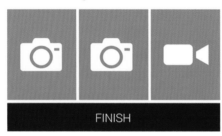

FINISH

Registration screen step 2

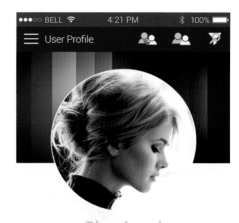

Blue Angel

Annie Doe, 15.06.1978

Interested in: Male

EDIT PROFILE

Profile screen

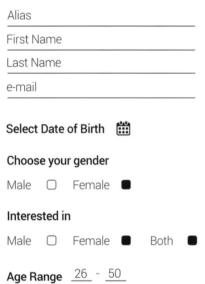

REGISTER AND CREATE PROFILE 1

SET SEARCH CRITERIA 2

SEND AND RECEIVE POKES 3

ASK FOR A DATE OR CALL 4

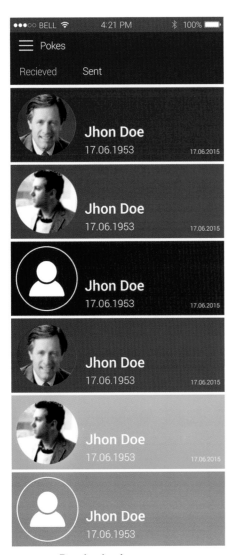

Received pokes screen

Matches screen

Send poke screen

Photo Camera	Video Camera	Ignore	Accept	Settings			
Call	Matches Inbox	Poke Inbox	Search Filter	Poke nearby	Edit	Edit Photo	Calendar

BRAIN DROPS

Designer: Danica Glodjovic   Country: Serbia

The main concept of Brain Drops app is to turn free or wasted time into productive time for business people. There are thousands of business people at the airport or railroad station waiting for a connection. They could use the app to meet people nearby with the same business ideas or similar interests and exchange their ideas. It also offers possibilities for making appointments, calls and chat, etc.

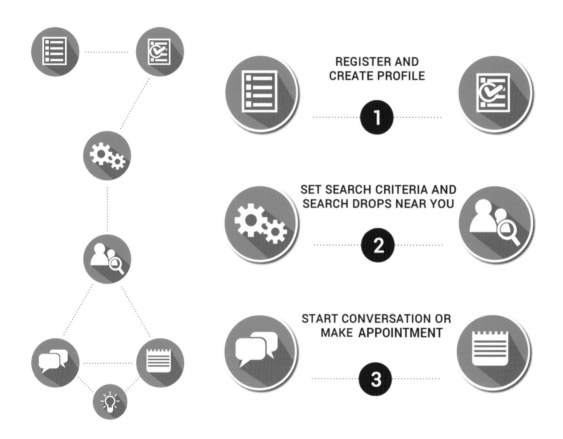

REGISTER AND
CREATE PROFILE
1

SET SEARCH CRITERIA AND
SEARCH DROPS NEAR YOU
2

START CONVERSATION OR
MAKE APPOINTMENT
3

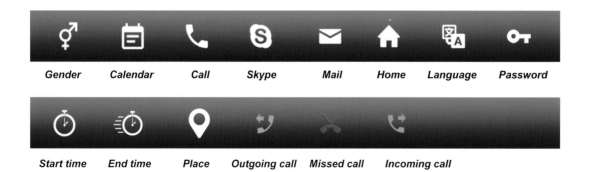

| *Gender* | *Calendar* | *Call* | *Skype* | *Mail* | *Home* | *Language* | *Password* |

| *Start time* | *End time* | *Place* | *Outgoing call* | *Missed call* | *Incoming call* |

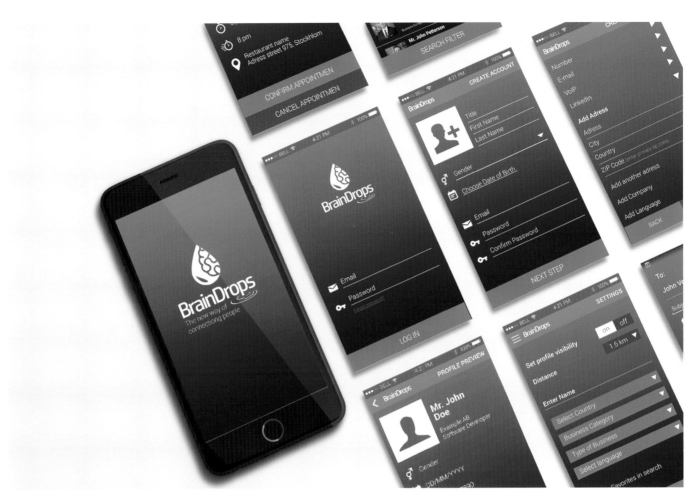

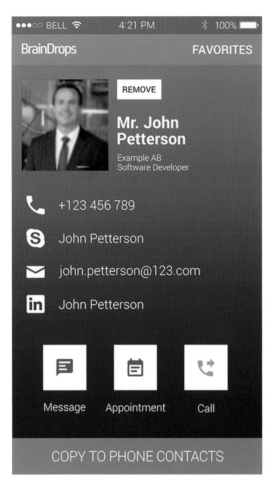

BrainDrops   FAVORITES

REMOVE

Mr. John Petterson

Example AB
Software Developer

📞 +123 456 789

Ⓢ John Petterson

✉ john.petterson@123.com

in John Petterson

💬 Message   📅 Appointment   📞 Call

COPY TO PHONE CONTACTS

favorite person screen

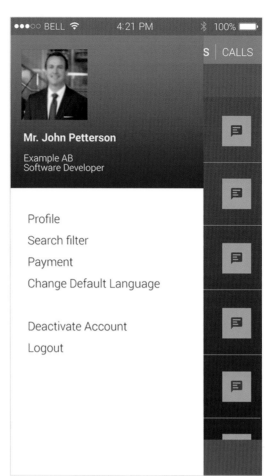

S | CALLS

Mr. John Petterson

Example AB
Software Developer

Profile

Search filter

Payment

Change Default Language

Deactivate Account

Logout

slide menu screen

BrainDrops   CREATE ACCOUNT

Title
First Name
Last Name

♂ Gender ▼

📅 Choose Date of Birth

✉ Email

🔑 Password

🔑 Confirm Password

NEXT STEP

VoIP (enter data) ➕ Viber ▼

LinkedIn ▼
jhon.doe@123.com

Add Adress ▼

Adress 1. Street adress No1
City Belgrade
Country Serbia
ZIP Code 11 000

Adress 2. Street adress No1
City Belgrade
Country Serbia
ZIP Code 11 000

Add another adress ➕

SAVE

BrainDrops   CREATE ACCOUNT

Number ▶
E-mail ▶
VoIP ▶
LinkedIn ▶

Add Adress ▼
Adress
City
Country
ZIP Code (enter primary zip code)

Add another adress ➕
Add Company ▶
Add Language ▶

BACK   FINISH

new message screen

search hits

make appointment

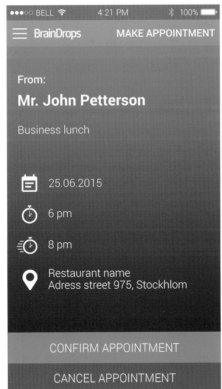

confirm appointment

ABOKI

Designer: Shabbir Manpurwala   Country: India

Aboki is an innovative platform for users to find people on a map and start chatting with them. Users can chat with a group or an individual and create their personal groups.

Thought Process

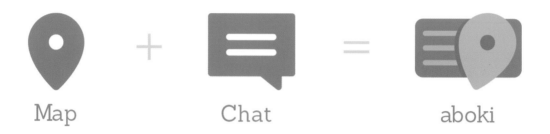

Map   +   Chat   =   aboki

Aboki Style Guidelines

UI Colors

#0098ff	#7536ff	#2dd635	#ff003c
#59517b	#a8a3c2	#e8e7ec	#ffffff

Font

Rubik (Google Fonts)

Font Size

36px
32px
28px
24px
20px

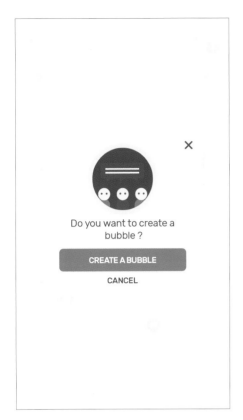

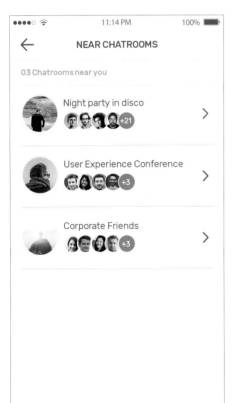

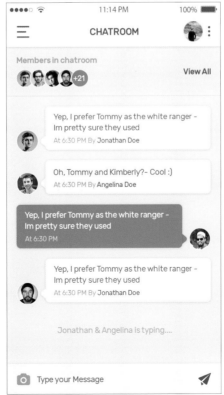

Bubbles l
Citizen --

· Pinch to zoom in / out
· Drag to scroll to other parts of the map
· Tap bubble to open chat room

· Long press to open extra options:
new private chat
request to kick
block user

· Minimize chat room / view next screen
· Also the same as swiping left/right to cycle through chat rooms and map (contemplating removing the button completely, since swiping does the same function)

· Close chat room. No additional notifications will be received from this room

· Invite a friend from your contact list to join the chat room (Feature only available to registered users)

CHAT ROOM 1

Anon1: Hello
Anon2: You don kolo
Anon3: Calm down. No vex.
Me: Chai, there is God ooo
Deadpool42: Baba go slow
Anon4: I am the truth
BWayne: I am batman

CHAT: BWayne

Me: Chai we need special prayers
BWayne: and some holy water

BWayne has left the room.

Rate User

★★★☆☆

· Each phone will keep track of the user ratings provided
· To keep ratings annonymous, XP updated once a day.
· 3 stars is +0 xp, 1 star is -2xp, 5 stars +2 xp, etc
· The person that initiates the private chat gets rated by the other user, i.e., a person that does not offer assistance by initiating private chats will not get any xp. Once a person "X" a private chat, they will no longer receive notifications.

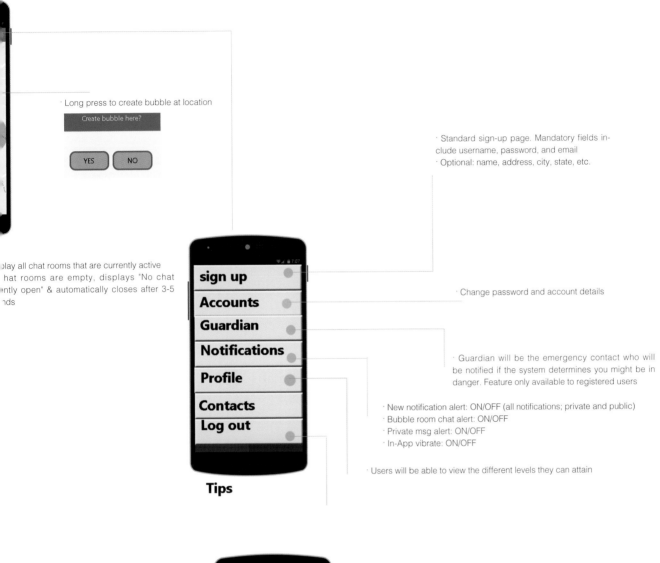

· Long press to create bubble at location

Create bubble here?

YES   NO

· Standard sign-up page. Mandatory fields include username, password, and email
· Optional: name, address, city, state, etc.

play all chat rooms that are currently active
hat rooms are empty, displays "No chat
intly open" & automatically closes after 3-5
nds

sign up

Accounts — · Change password and account details

Guardian

Notifications

Profile

Contacts

Log out

· Guardian will be the emergency contact who will be notified if the system determines you might be in danger. Feature only available to registered users

· New notification alert: ON/OFF (all notifications; private and public)
· Bubble room chat alert: ON/OFF
· Private msg alert: ON/OFF
· In-App vibrate: ON/OFF

· Users will be able to view the different levels they can attain

Tips

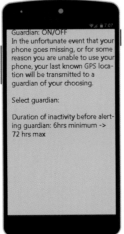

Guardian: ON/OFF
In the unfortunate event that your phone goes missing, or for some reason you are unable to use your phone, your last known GPS location will be transmitted to a guardian of your choosing.

Select guardian:

Duration of inactivity before alerting guardian: 6hrs minimum -> 72 hrs max

GROUPEEZ

Designer: Aloïs Castanino   Country: France

Groupeez is an iOS app that helps you find movie buddies. Users could discover films to watch with fellow movie lovers on Groupeezz, which is a social network that gets you talking and helps you arrange to see films together. Clear calls to action and a streamlined chat function make it easy for groups to form around movie screenings. The friendly, minimalistic and colorful interface is combined with illustration plus traditional flat design. Branded illustrations were also used to onboard new users.

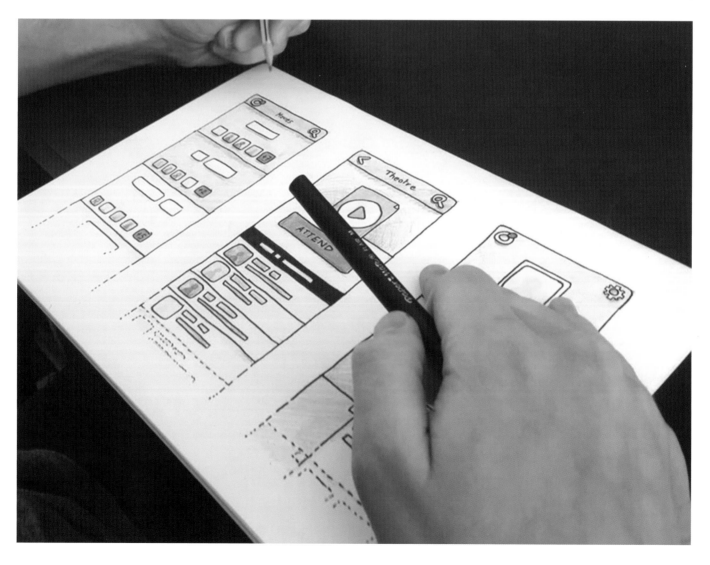

ONBOARDING – DATING APP

Designer: Soong Sup Shin   Country: United States

In this dating app's welcome screens, we communicate in a fun and playful way through a series of interconnected animations. The animations along with the bold pastel color scheme gives the app a strong, branded personality, even though the layout is very clean and simple. The designers believe that this approach gives a great first impression to new users before they enter the app.

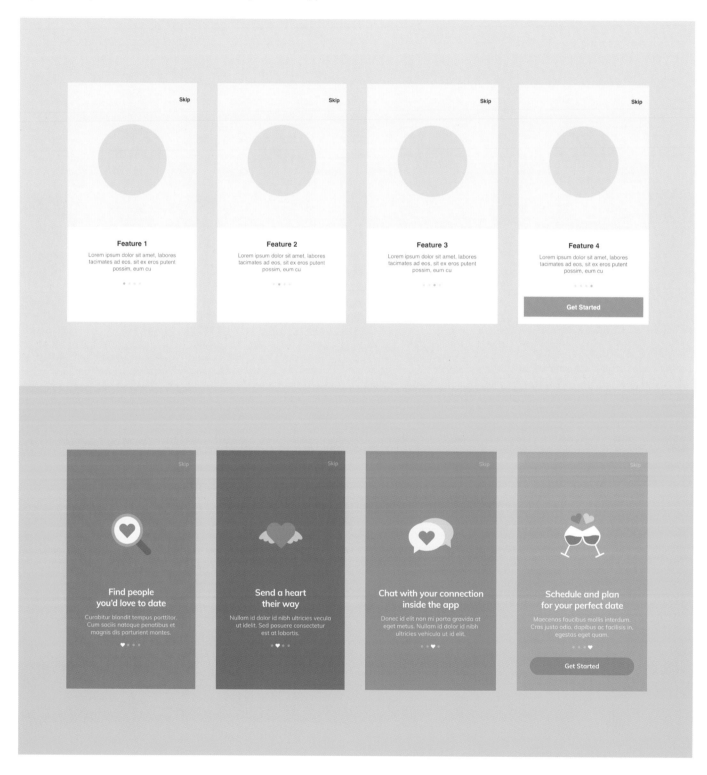

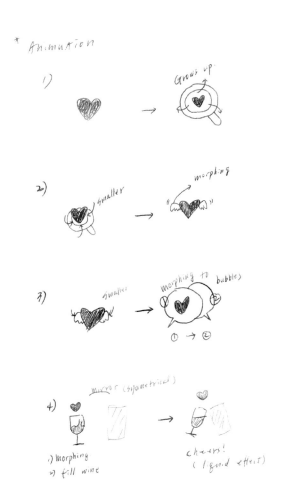

* Animation

1)
Grows up.

2)
smaller   morphing

3)
smaller   morphing to bubble)
① → ②

4)
mirror (symmetrical)
) morphing
) fill wine
cheers!
(liquid effect)

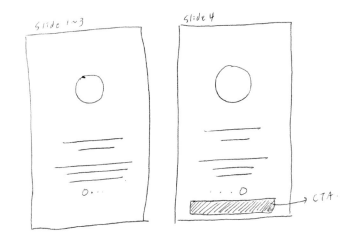

Slide 1~3   Slide 4
O...   . . . O
CTA.

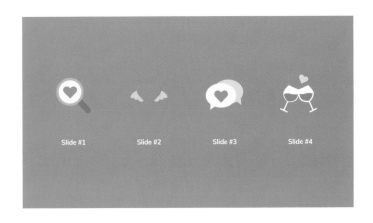

Slide #1   Slide #2   Slide #3   Slide #4

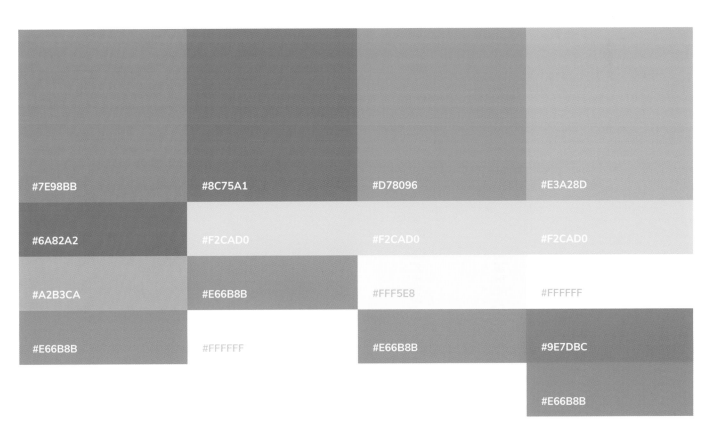

#7E98BB	#8C75A1	#D78096	#E3A28D
#6A82A2	#F2CAD0	#F2CAD0	#F2CAD0
#A2B3CA	#E66B8B	#FFF5E8	#FFFFFF
#E66B8B	#FFFFFF	#E66B8B	#9E7DBC
			#E66B8B

TOOWAY

Designer: Taehee Kim, Hyemin Yoo   Country: Germany / South Korea

TOOWAY app service was created to help people with making decisions. Users can vote anonymously on whether they think a choice might be right or wrong and post a problem to be evaluated by fellow users.

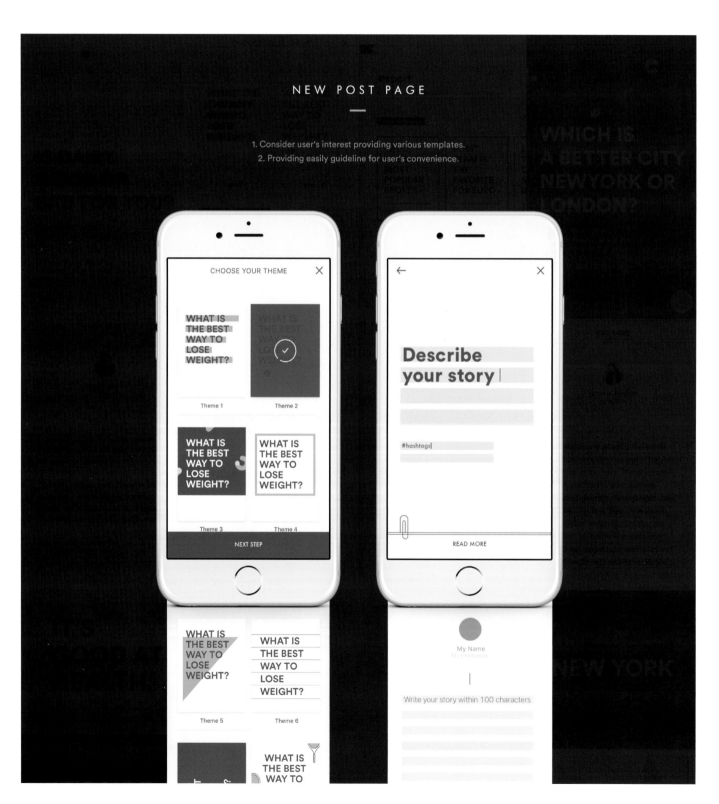

POSTING PAGE

—

1. Providing visual consistent with scroll screen
2. Delivering visual pleasure with changing pattern depending on hashtag.
3. Delivering visual pleasure while swiping motion of two choices.

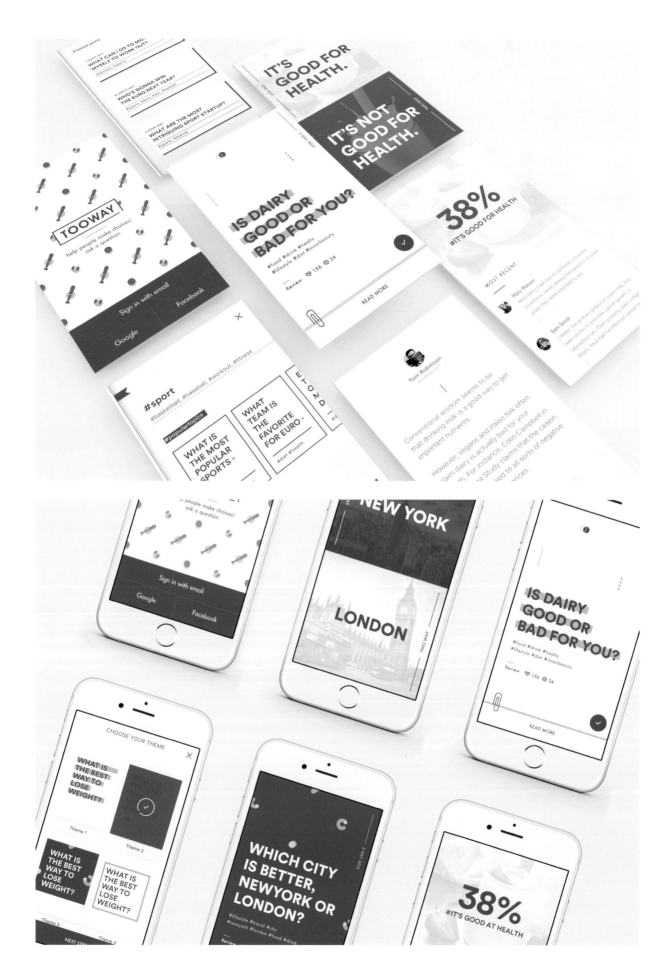

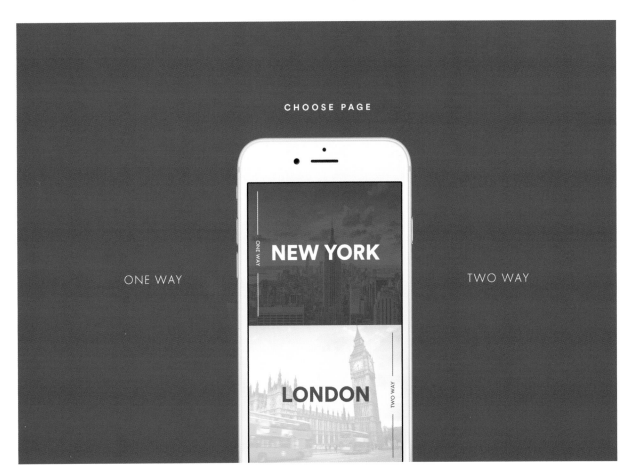

CHOOSE PAGE

ONE WAY

NEW YORK

ONE WAY

LONDON

TWO WAY

TWO WAY

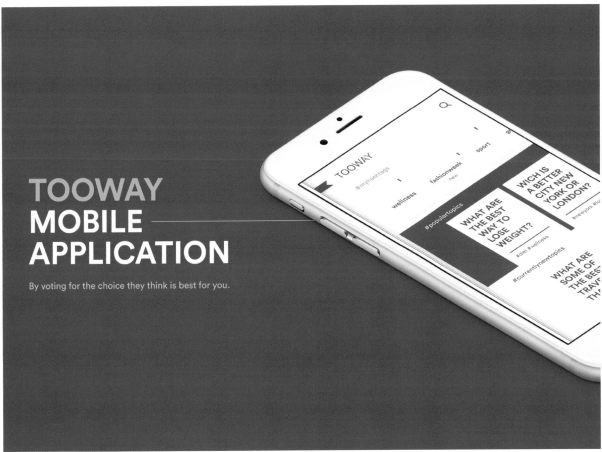

TOOWAY
MOBILE
APPLICATION

By voting for the choice they think is best for you.

ENGAGEMENT IN INTERACTION DESIGN

Annelies Clauwaert
Belgium
Art Director

Understanding human psychology goes a long way when it comes to design in general. Designs that have a human touch just feel right. There are a variety of ways to conceive an emotional experience. Color, contrast, images, fonts, composition can create a specific mood that fits the product. They don't add up to an emotion, but put together they can compose the right feeling. Of course interaction design is not only about establishing an emotional connection and having the right atmosphere, your design should satisfy specific needs and desires of the potential users. After all, they are using your product for a reason.

In a fast-paced world like today, people don't want to work or think more than they have to. Users want to reach their goals as fast as possible, without any friction. **This brings us to the nature of interaction design, engagement.** Technology used to create a need for design, so people would be able to interact with newly created devices. It all started with making familiar and intuitive interfaces based on a few key elements of cognitive psychology that are particularly valued in interaction design.

Affordances, interface metaphors, mental models... Think of the things you will find on pretty much every computer a trash can, calendar, e-mail, notes, folders, ... They are all based on a physical objects. The reason why these digital interfaces are trying to mimic objects we're familiar with is because human nature is something we're stuck with. Okay, that might sound a bit harsh, but it is true.

We can control technology, we can control design, but we can't control how people think and behave. Design acts like some kind of bridge between change and humanity. That change was, up till now, mostly driven by technology, but the world is changing quickly, and design is catching up. Design isn't just a tool anymore and the experience is growing to be more and more important. In the future, the lines between different types of designers will most likely start to blur, or even disappear. While we can't predict the future, we can prepare for it by keeping an eye on what's happening in the world, how users want to see digital information delivered, how they want to experience it and how designers can influence and support those changes.

FANZONE
Designer: Annelies Clauwaert

Fanzone is a Swedish company that provides digital solutions to professional athletes worldwide to manage their social media and monetise their fanbase. But with a focus on letting the athletes create an honest, spontaneous and unique fan relationship. This project consisted of 3 major parts: a rework of Fanzone's already existing brand identity, user experience optimisation of the iOS app and a completely new user interface design.

The main goal was to provide the users with an app that would save them time and puts them in control. This was accomplished by simplifying the user experience and placing the main feature - creating social media posts - in the spotlight. All other features were moved to the background to support this main action. Giving people more than they need just clutters up the experience.

Wireframes

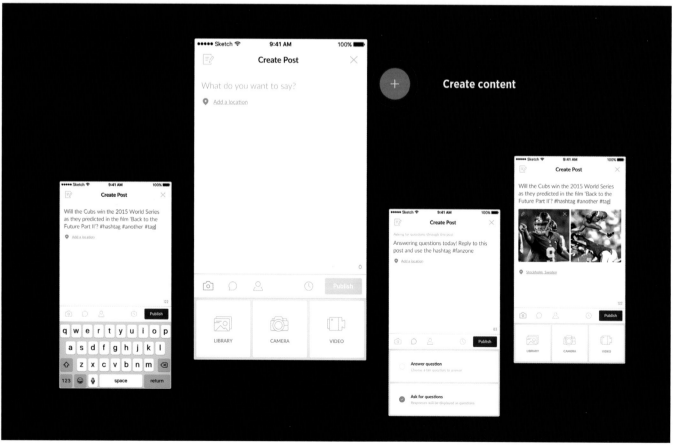

Create content

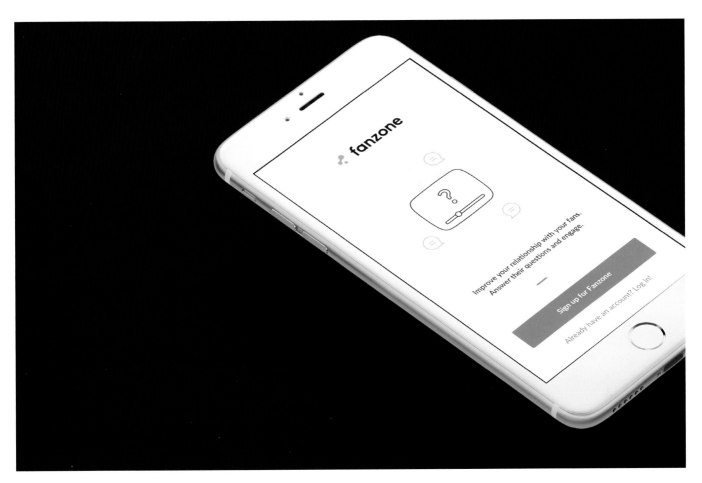

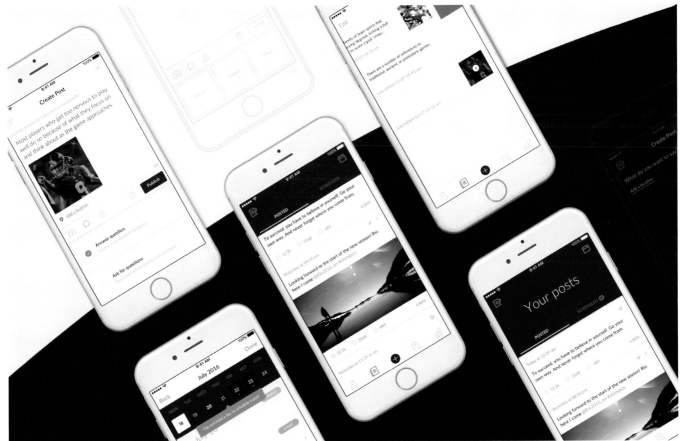

053

TEXTMATE

Designer: Fahad Basil   Country: United Arab Emirates

TextMate offers a simple, elegant way for you to reach your client base through text message marketing. Their promise is simple: send messages to anywhere in the world for one affordable rate.

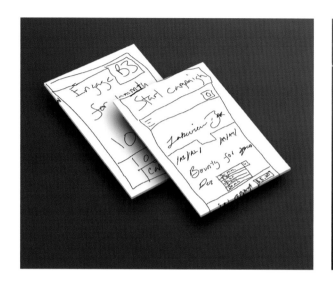

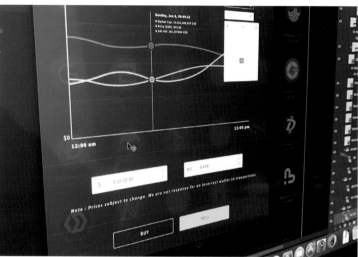

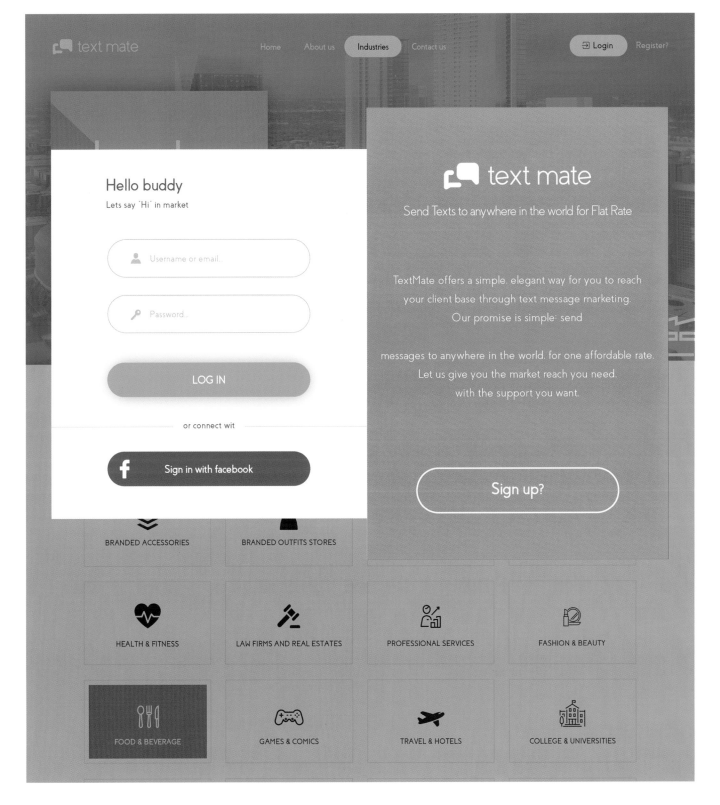

DESTINO

Designer: Nguyễn Hồng Hạnh   Country: Vietnam

Destino is specially designed for your next mobile dating application. It is an anonymous dating app template with 60+ iOS screens which are easy to edit in the Photoshop, Adobe XD and Sketch.

Logo Concept

Wireframe & User Flow

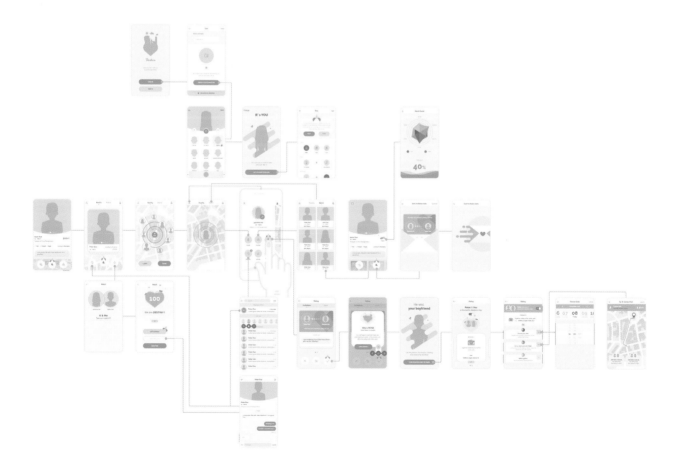

Prototype

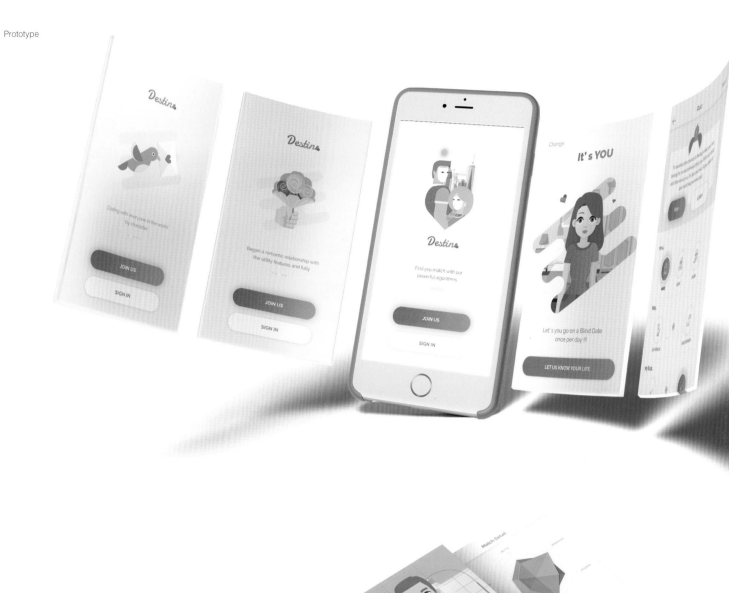

SHALLO

Designer: Mostafa Amharrar   Country: Morocco

The Shallo project is a very creative and clean design for building applications. This UI template is designed for iOS mobile devices and presented in a lovely mockup using Adobe Photoshop.

●●●○○ Carrier 📶   1:20 PM   ✈ ✶ 100% ▬

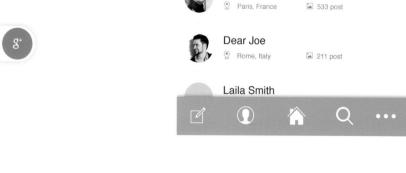

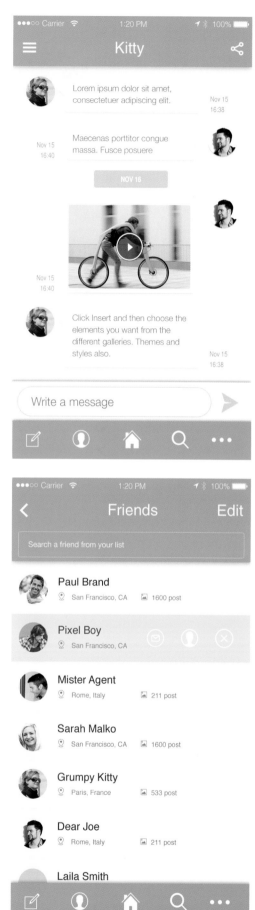

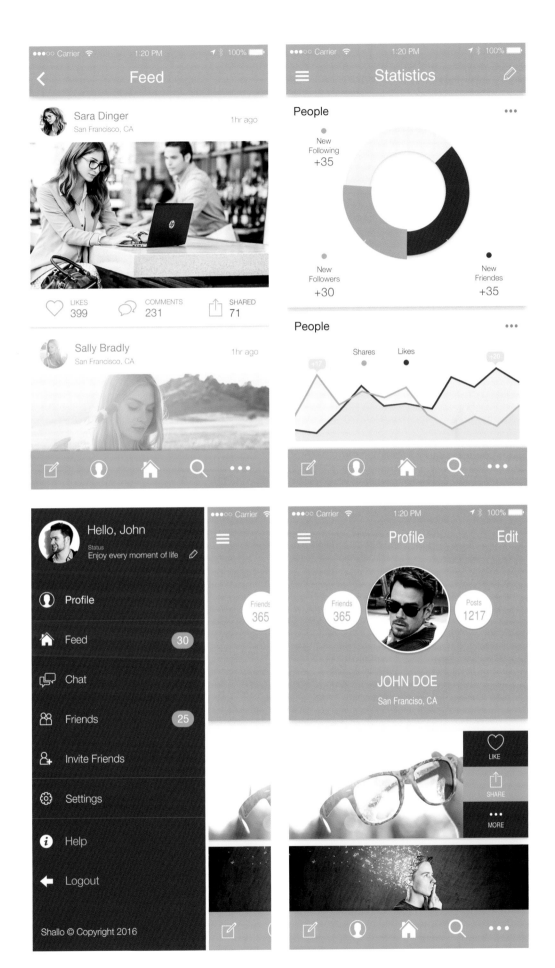

RECREATIONAL
INTERACTION DESIGN

Various kinds of mobile apps enrich people's daily lives. How do designers apply the principles of interaction design to satisfy users' leisure needs?

GAMES

 AUDIOVISUAL INTERACTION

 DIGITAL MAGAZINES

LEARNING THROUGH INTERACTIVE STORYTELLING

Fabian Gampp
Germany
Multidisciplinary Designer

The idea of the interactive learning environment is based on the well-established read-aloud technique, which is often used in kindergartens and primary schools, where the teacher reads a story for a group of children. By visualizing the story in real-time and enabling the children to interact, Gundula's stories add another layer to this setup. All the technological elements are hidden within the wooden tortoise to not interrupt the interaction between the children and the teacher. In that way, it is possible to create magic moments and to enrich the whole storytelling experience.

To address children in a playful and appealing way, storytelling is very important. In the case of the interactive learning environment, the wooden tortoise (Gundula) creates an emotional connection between the children and the story. They accompany Gundula on a journey to find a new friend. During their journey, they learn about the characteristics of the four seasons and get to know a lot of animals. Along the way, Gundula has to solve challenges in which the children can interact with their movements and their voices. Since the tortoise can also be used as a toy without the projection, it is easy to implement it in their daily routine.

Our children grow up in a digitized world in which technology is omnipresent. To catch up to these developments, schools started to equip their students with tablet computers and install digital whiteboards in the classrooms. However, the old learning software doesn't suit the needs of the students or is not easy to implement in normal teaching practice. Technology-driven solutions can disrupt relationships between the students and their teacher and thereby hinder good learning experiences. Therefore, we need to design software, toys and games which are based on the needs of children and are deeply rooted in the context of their learning situation. Thoughtfully created interaction design is then able to build a bridge between the children and technology, which offers inspiration, empowers them and promotes their creativity.

GUNDULA'S STORIES

Designer: Fabian Gampp

Gundula's stories is an interactive learning environment which enables children to acquire knowledge playfully and improve their sensory and motor skills. The learning environment combines classical storytelling with technologies such as gesture control and voice recognition. Designed for usage in kindergartens and primary schools, it consists of a character made out of wood (Gundula the tortoise) with an integrated Kinect sensor, a beamed projection that brings to life an illustrated story and a tablet application for the teacher to read and control the story flow.

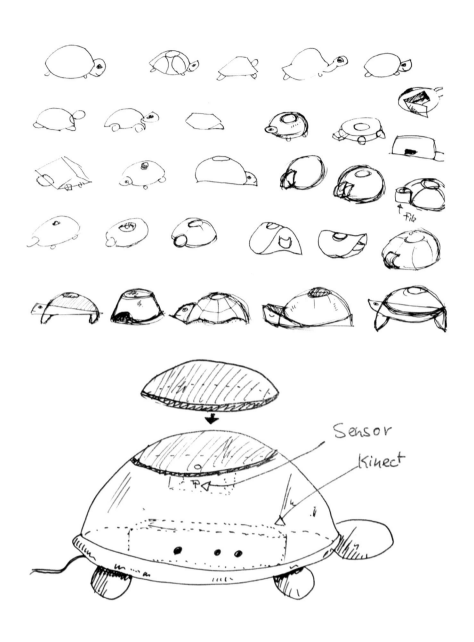

Sensor
Kinect

Der Sommer

Während Gundula durch die Blumenfelder und Wiesen läuft wird es immer heißer und heißer. „Wenn es so heiß ist, muss es wohl schon Sommer geworden sein," denkt Gundula. Auf einmal hört sie ein lautes Summen. „Kinder, wisst ihr vielleicht was das für ein Summen ist?"

Auf einer Sonnenblume direkt über Gundula sitzt eine kleine Biene. „Hallo Biene, ist das nicht ein wunderschöner Tag heute!" sagt Gundula fröhlich. Die Biene antwortet: „Ja, das Wetter ist schön aber ich bin traurig. Ich habe mich heute Morgen verflogen, als ich Nektar suchen wollte. Und jetzt finde ich nicht mehr nach Hause. Die Anderen vermissen mich bestimmt schon. Kannst du mir vielleicht helfen, wieder zurück nach Hause zu finden?"

Gundula überlegt ein bisschen und sagt: „Ja, gerne ich kann es versuchen. Vielleicht siehst du von da oben ja auch, ob sich zwischen den Sonnenblumen eine Schildkröte versteckt. Gundula sagt zu den Kindern: "Lasst uns versuchen, der Biene den Heimweg zu zeigen." Interaktion Bewegung: Folge ⌒ eichelten Linie um die Biene nach Hause zu bringen.

☹ 😐 ☺

Die vier Jahreszeiten

Der Frühling

Auf ihrem Weg bemerkt Gundula, wie das Gras immer grüner wird und die Vögel in den verschiedensten Tonarten zu singen beginnen. „Das muss der Frühling sein, so schön ist nur der Frühling", denkt Gundula. Nachdem Sie eine Weile unterwegs ist, kommt sie an einen Teich. Gundula schaut sich um, ob sie eine andere Schildkröte entdeckt. Aber dort sitzt nur ein kleiner Frosch, der aufgeregt auf und ab hüpft. „Hallo kleiner Frosch, wie geht es dir?" fragt Gundula. „Nicht so gut", erwidert der Frosch traurig. „Es ist jetzt schon so lange Frühling, aber es hat noch kein bisschen geregnet. Schau, der Teich, er ist fast ausgetrocknet. Wenn so wenig Wasser darin ist, kann ich dort mit meinen kleinen Kaulquappen nicht leben. Auch die Blumen scheinen immer noch zu schlafen, obwohl sie schon längst aus dem Boden hätten kommen müssen. Gundula, kannst du mir vielleicht helfen?" Gundula antwortet zögerlich: "Obje, ich weiß nicht ob ich das schaffe. ____ leicht können dir meine

»Helfe dem Frosch regen zu machen indem du auf das Zauberlicht stehst und mit deiner Hand die Wolke über die Blumen ziehst«

☹ 😐 ☺

Die vier Jahreszeiten

WHEN INTERACTION MEETS FURNITURE

THINKING INTERACTIVE
China
Interaction Design Studio

Future interaction will let users experience an optimized virtual furniture flagship store

In the future, technology will be closely related to interaction design. And interaction design will incorporate more VR&3D technologies. A good question is: "How to display unlimited product possibilities in a limited retail store". We try to explore more possibilities of interaction display based on customer demands. Our solution is to create a digitalized flagship store with 3D images and interaction language on an iPad. The combination of virtual experience and a commercial entity gives us more possibilities to develop business strategy.

The 3D scenario experience gives consumers an unparalleled immersive experience. Furniture becomes a family member rather than an object. Selling furniture becomes more like selling a lifestyle. Interaction design changes traditional modes of one-way information transmitting. Customers will actively know more about the information. A new mode of communication between stores and customers will be established. The communication barrier will be broken in a scenarized interaction process.

Interesting interaction makes products and ideas known to more people

Furniture is a creation. Every good creation has its unique charm in the idea, imagination and style. How to communicate the hidden message behind the products to consumers?

Interaction is a dialogue between users and products. Users gain knowledge of the product from the usability, touch control and gestures, etc. The designers use motion image to illustrate implicit design concepts. The intangible conception will be turned into tangible experience. Users will perceive, understand and imagine the products from the textures and structures, etc. Meanwhile, they will sense the hidden value of the product and gain interest in it. As a result, more and more good products will be known to people through interesting interaction processes.

QUMEI

Design Studio: THINKING INTERACTIVE

"QU MEI" app creatively uses a three-dimensional exhibition method by providing authentic 3D sample space. The 3D furniture can be rotated in 720 degrees, helping users searching for their desired furniture. Users can enjoy the pleasure of online shopping with the app.

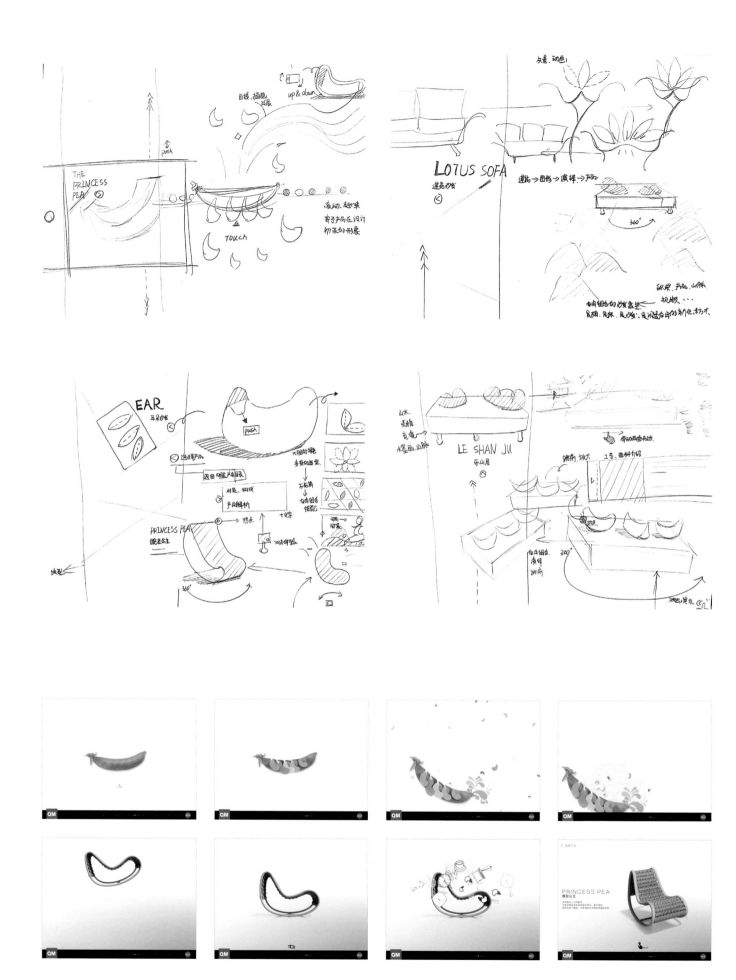

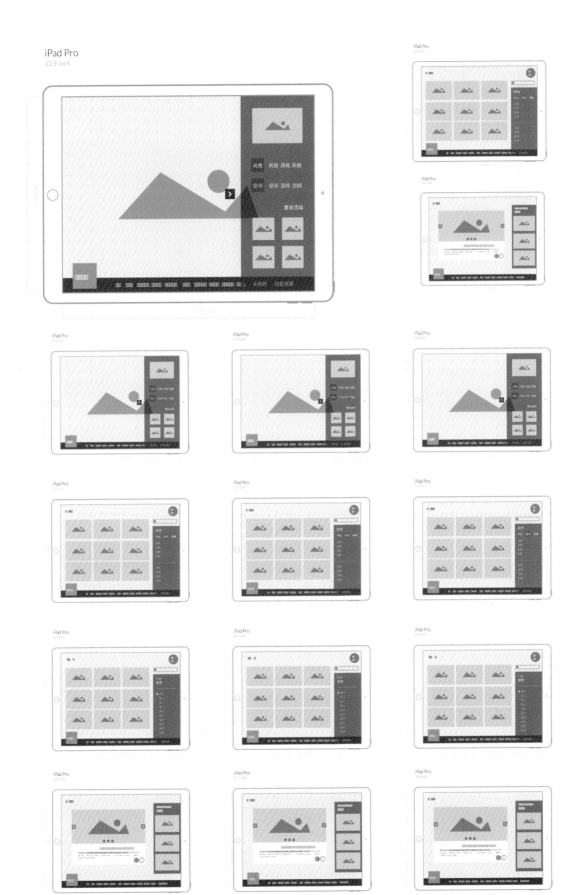

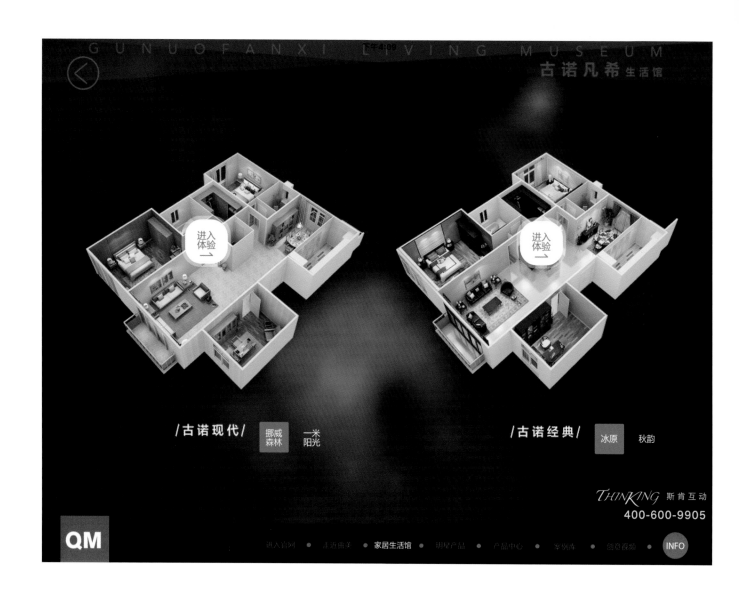

FEELOO

Designer: Dubosquet Sebastien   Country: France

FEELOO is an easy game to pick up and to play for all ages with increasing challenges along the way. There are thirty amazing and colorful levels for users to play!

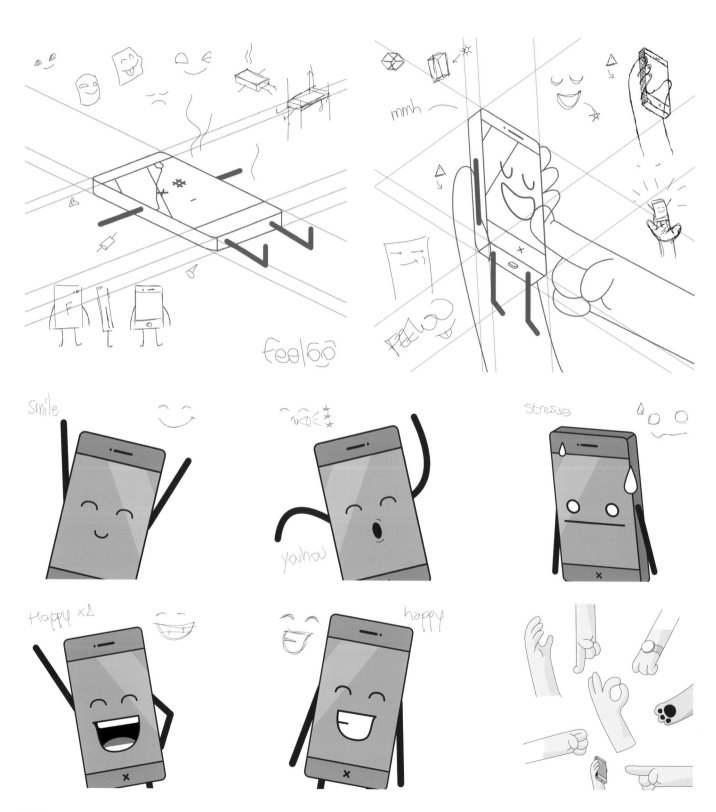

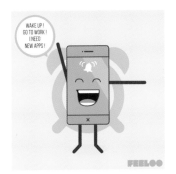
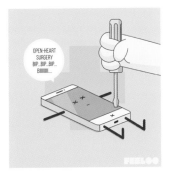

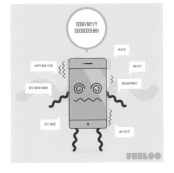

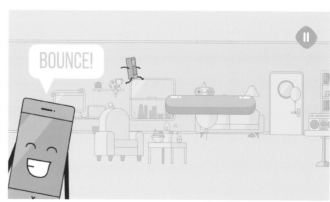

SPEEDER

Designer: Turgay Mutlay   Country: Turkey

Speeder is a funny game. Users will be the captain. Their task is to collect the gems by avoiding the different obstacles. It provides different spaceships for users to unlock and play.

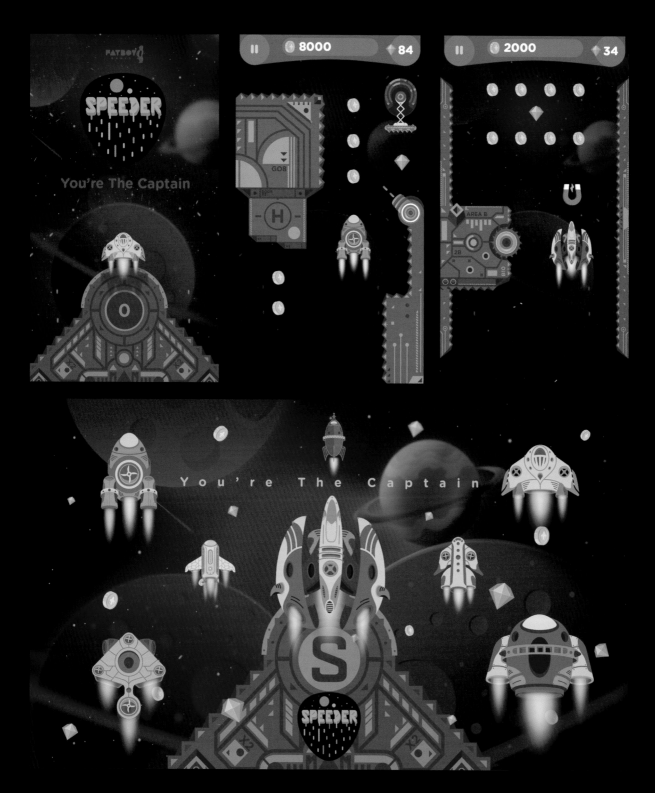

SWAT CRAFT

AIR CRAFT

TIRO CRAFT

STINGRAYS CRAFT

HAWK CRAFT

BAZOOKA CRAFT

DRONE CRAFT

HOWER CRAFT

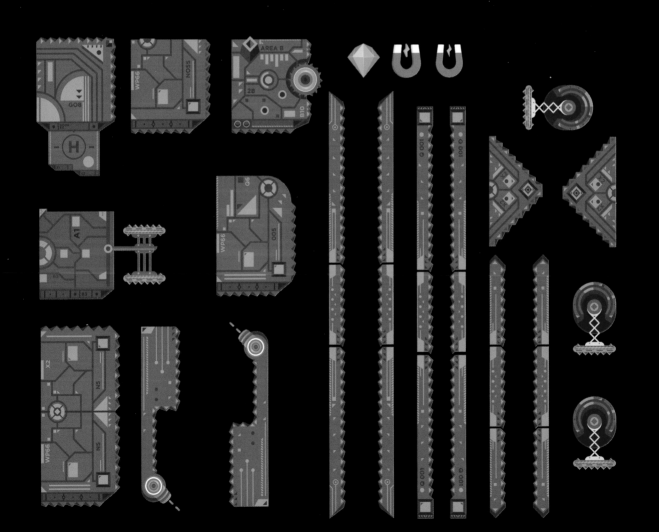

RACCOO

Design: Inkration Studio   Country: United Kingdom

RACCOO is a mobile game for the platformer fans. It is an atmosphere game about a nocturnal animal, who is beating the obstacles in night jungles of Amazoka. He meets different opponents on his way, from the usual mosquito to the royal alligator. The uniqueness of this game is in its atmosphere locations, details that are formed with help of silhouette interplay and various light spots.

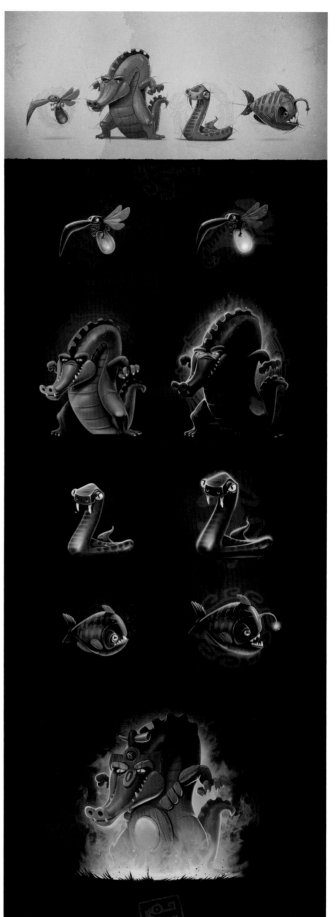

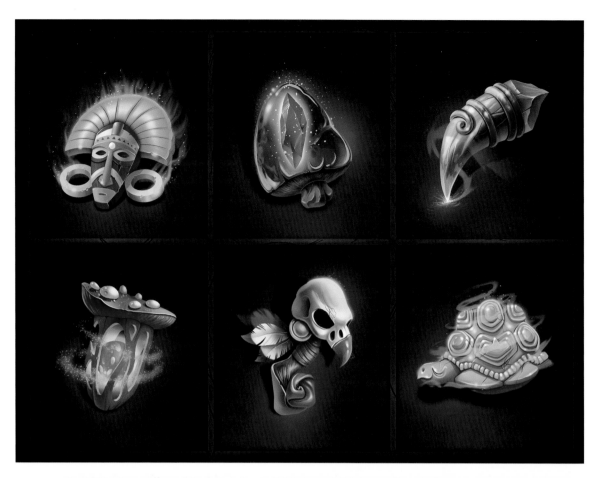

TWIST THE GEAR

Design: Inkration Studio   Country: United Kingdom

The designers' goal was to create something new in popular slots games. They decided to give them a new vision with the help of an interesting scrip, which revolves around Professor Garold. Professor has invented a new source of energy, which the main antagonist character Spike wants to steal. The professor creates a robot to protect the source of energy from Spike. Along with the standard slot game, the player has to collect robot details and go through bonus games. An interesting script and additional mini games make this game different from other slots games.

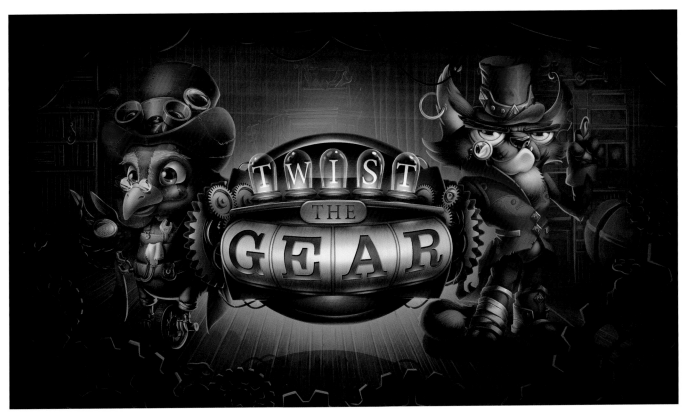

A BEAR'S-EYE VIEW OF YELLOWSTONE

Designer: Andreas Anderskou   Client: National Geographic   Country: United States

Follow the journeys of four bears navigating the heart of Yellowstone, as seen from the bears' own point of view. This groundbreaking research that attaches cameras to bears gives us a lens into the never-before-seen lives of one of the animal kingdom's most fearsome beasts.

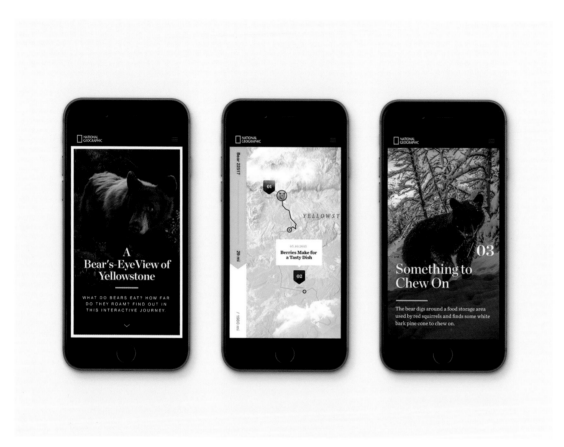

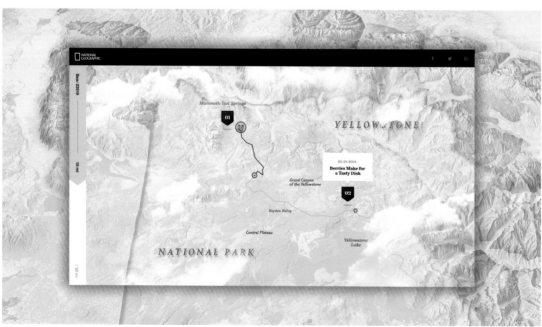

Bear loader walk-cycle
Black

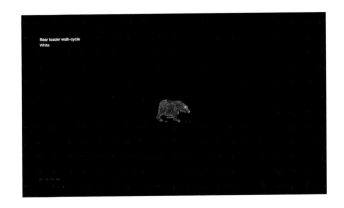

Bear loader walk-cycle
White

Bear loader walk-cycle
Walk cycle key frames

Keys   **01**   02   03   **04**   05   06   **07**   08   09   **10**

National Geographic
Illustration board

INTERACTIVE DESIGN EVOLVES ALONG WITH TECHNOLOGY

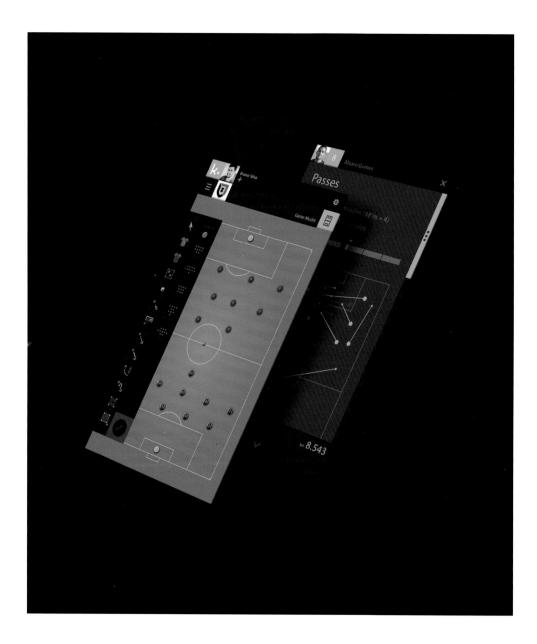

Bruno Miguel Silva
Portugal
Art Director
Interaction Designer
Graphic Designer

To obtain the greatest success possible in the field of interaction design, we have to know our user on all human levels. The psychological and emotional knowledge of the user is very important because it leads us to make better choices and decisions for our work, then our understanding and connection will be higher. Therefore, the greater the connection and empathy of the user to the service/product, the more he feels comfortable in using it. And this comfort/ link is vital to the success of the interaction.

Understanding users' motivations, weaknesses and skills help us to create interaction and content that is perceived and makes sense to users. The emotional connection helps us to achieve a more effective interaction and a more tolerant relationship. It is very important to have a real relationship between users and product/service.

We must understand the behaviors and relationships of our users. We have to know their routines, addictions, etc. This process will help us to create interaction models that are familiar and easy to assimilate. Communication patterns are easily created through this learning process.

To achieve good transmission of information in interactive design, it is necessary to know the user on a cultural level. Their language, traditions and customs have to be studied and understood in order to understand the meaning of the colors, images, shapes and symbols have for users, so we can interact/communicate correctly. This knowledge is the basis of all communication; it is impossible to convey the information correctly and get an effective interaction without this knowledge.

The best way to communicate with people is always the interest of the subject/content in common. Besides, things with which people identify also results in approach and this bring interaction. Communication between people and the machine goes in the same direction, that is, the more features in common, the more

likely they are to have a successful interaction.

In the future, we will navigate virtual reality and have many experiences. It is a recent field and can be quite interesting. I also hope to see some progress by Apple in the near future for its operating systems. **Our interaction will increasingly be aided by animations.**

Interaction design is an evolution and learning process that always depends on the media and technology in which it is or is developed and also the knowledge that the user has of the technological and interactive world. Knowing that the interaction must always respect and evolve with the user's knowledge level, educate the user slowly so they don't feel disoriented. It is important to hear feedback from users to enable the interaction to evolve in the right direction.

The goal of interaction design is always to serve the user, helping them to understand and communicate more effectively and comfortably in an ever more positive experience.

TATIK

Designer: Bruno Miguel Silva

Tatik is an application and social network for the football world. It promises to manage and structure the football clubs, helping coaches to have control over all aspects of the game. Tools for managing, analysing, scouting, game models, tracking systems and training editors are some of the topics included.

The specialized social network with different profiles are created for professional players, amateur players, clubs, fans, sports newspapers and reporters, meeting their unique needs and providing a dynamic and exciting environment for the audience.

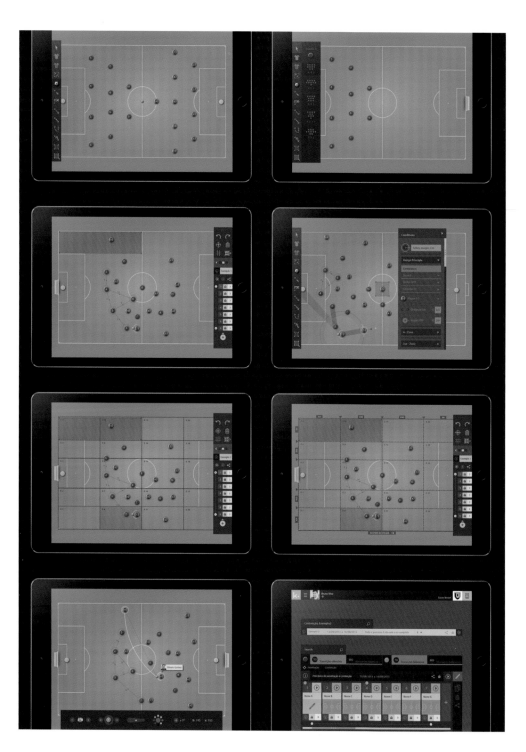

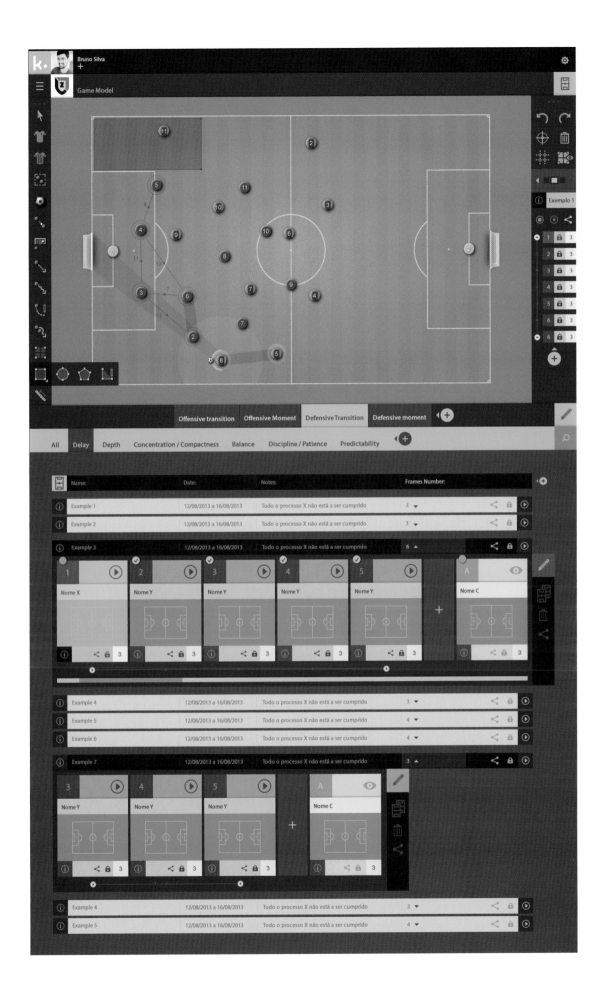

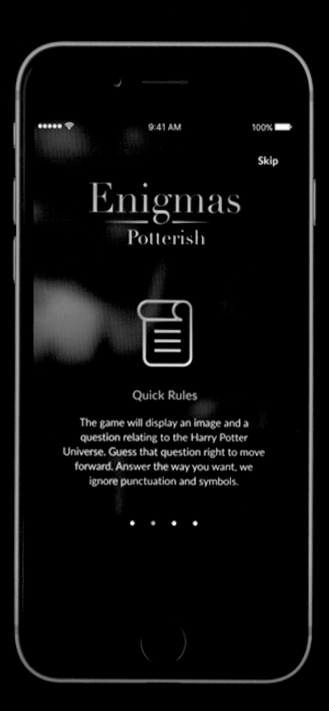

ENIGMAS POTTERISH

Designer: Victor Berbel   Country: Brazil

Enigmas Potterish is a trivia game app that uses time for its mechanics. Each challenge has a timer on top and the user who accomplishes more challenges in less time gets a higher score on the overall ranking. The game is available in three languages, namely, Portuguese, English and Spanish. The user can only play three challenges a day, so this is for real Harry Potter fans.

Before   After

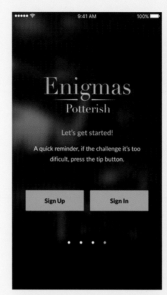

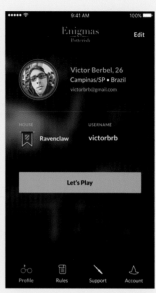

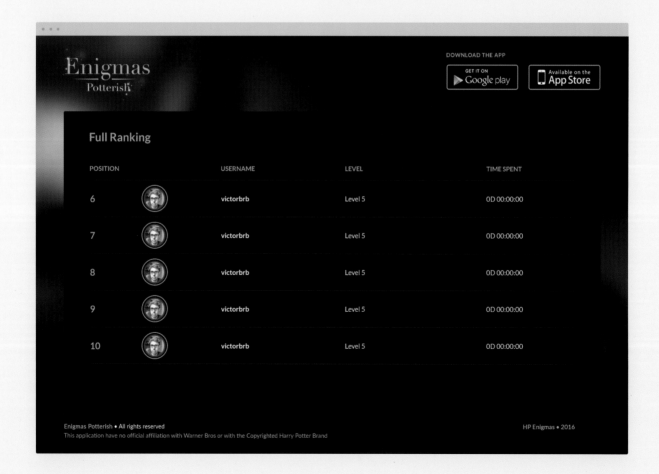

Profile

Rules

Support

Account

No Tip Left

No Tips Left

You have to resolve this on your own.

Ok

9:41 AM

Enigmas
Potterish

Victor Berbel, 26
Campinas/SP • Brazil
victorbrb@gmail.com

USERNAME
victorbrb

HOUSE
Ravenclaw

Let's Play

100%

Done

Profile

9:41 AM

Enigmas
Potterish

FULL NAME
Insert your name here

AGE
00

USERNAME
Type username

E-MAIL
victorbrb@gmail.com

100%

9:41 AM

Enigmas
Potterish

Settings

Rules

Support

CONNECT SOCIAL ACCOUNTS

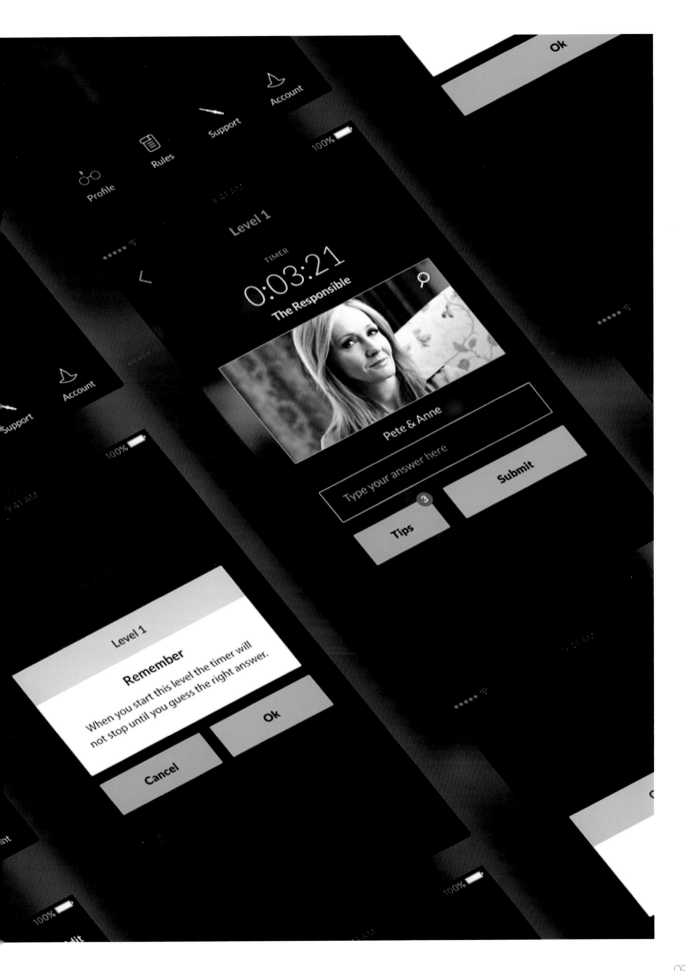

BALLOONS IN THE SKY

Designer: Anna Zwolińska   Country: United Kingdom

"Balloons in the Sky" is an endless arcade game. It surprises players with a unique graphical style which you won't find in any other game. The goal is simple - survive as long as possible while avoiding balloons and collecting special items. Despite simple mechanics, the game uses unusual solutions. Multiple locations and sceneries were designed to give different experiences by using custom mechanics and different difficulty levels.

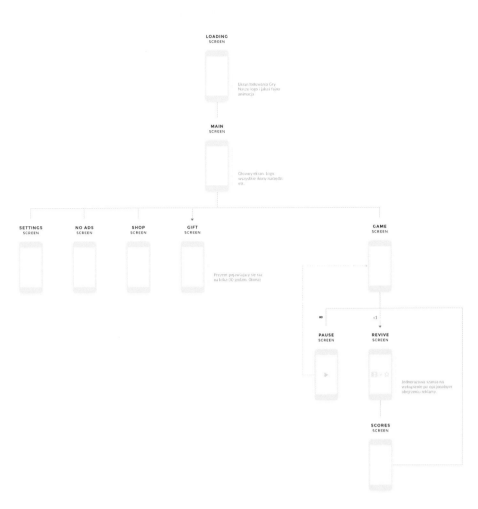

LOADING
SCREEN

Ekran ładowania Gry.
Nasze logo i jakaś fajna
animacja

MAIN
SCREEN

Głowny ekran. Logo
wszystkie ikony narzędzi
etc.

SETTINGS
SCREEN

NO ADS
SCREEN

SHOP
SCREEN

GIFT
SCREEN

GAME
SCREEN

Przerw pojawiający się raz
na kilka (X) godzin. (Ikona)

∞

<1

PAUSE
SCREEN

REVIVE
SCREEN

Jednorazowa szansa na
wykupienie po opcjonalnym
obejrzeniu reklamy.

SCORES
SCREEN

FALLEN STAR FM

Designer: Dmitriy Zhernovnikov   Country: Ukraine

This app is for radio fans. They can listen to music, add their favorite stations, songs, and share those with friends and always be in touch with the latest news.

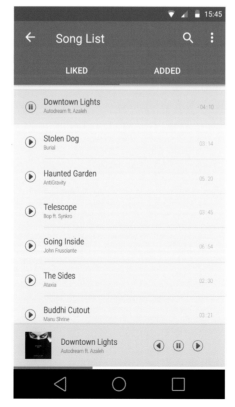

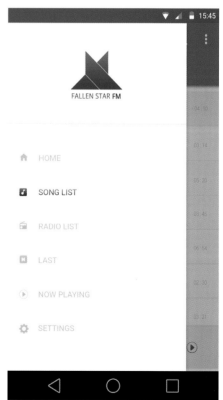

USER EXPERIENCE

User Experience of the app is pretty simple and user-friendly.
There are no excess details or elements, only the most important functionality.

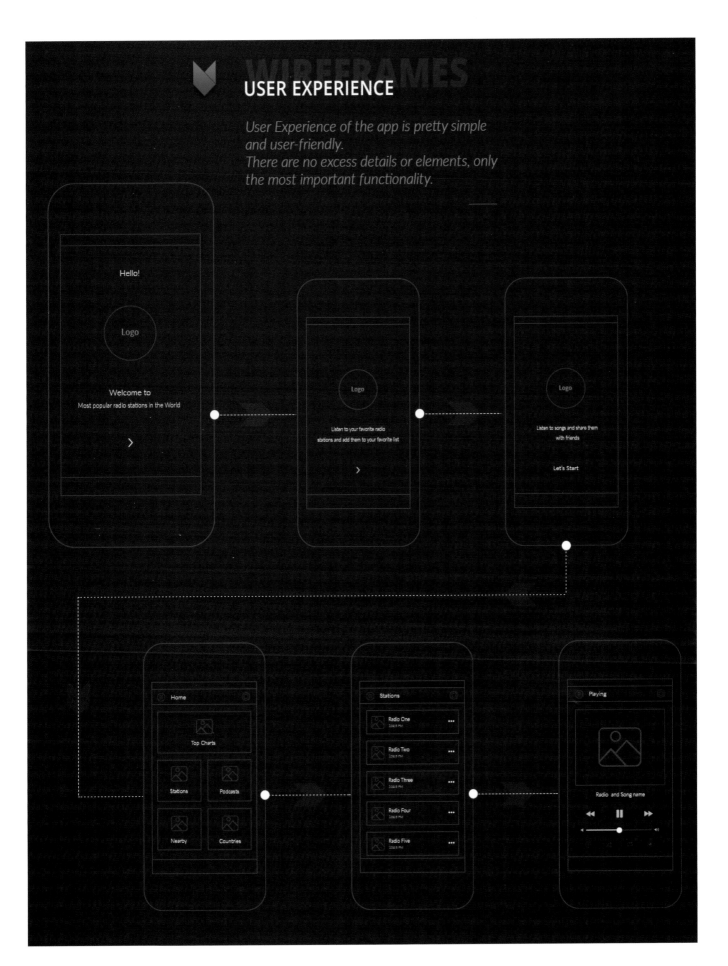

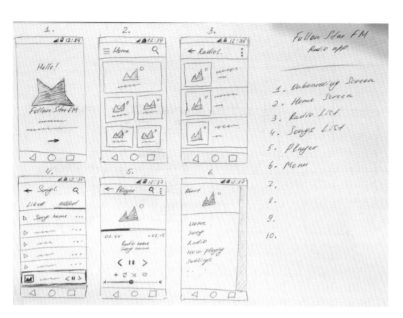

Fallen Star FM
Radio app.

1. Onboarding Screen
2. Home Screen
3. Radio List
4. Songs List
5. Player
6. Menu
7.
8.
9.
10.

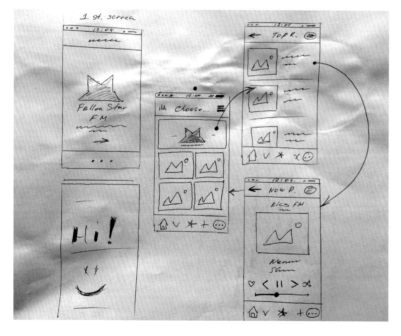

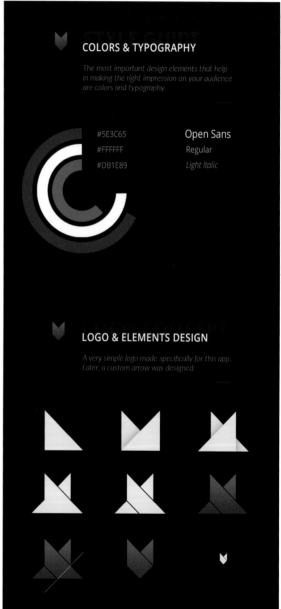

COLORS & TYPOGRAPHY

The most important design elements that help
in making the right impression on your audience
are colors and typography.

#5E3C65   Open Sans
#FFFFFF   Regular
#DB1E89   Light Italic

LOGO & ELEMENTS DESIGN

A very simple logo made specifically for this app.
Later, a custom arrow was designed.

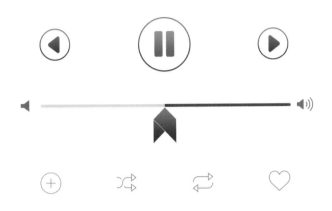

FALLEN STAR **FM**

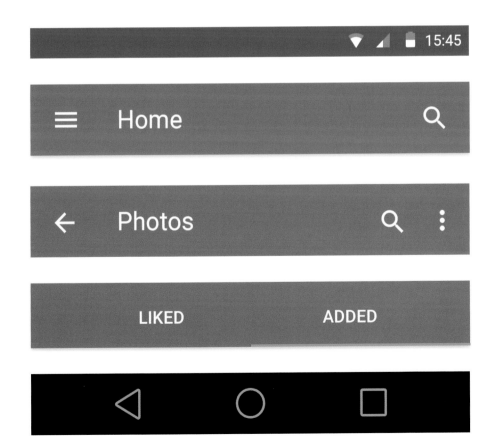

INTERACTION DESIGN PRINCIPLES THAT BOOST USER ENGAGEMENT

Every landing page is designed to provide a specific value and its goal is to get visitors who appreciate that value to perform interaction with the site. That includes sign up, buy and subscribe, etc. If people just visit your website and then leave without any interaction, it means your website doesn't offer any value or benefit that relates to them.

User engagement is measured as conversion rate - the percentage of users who take a desired action. In addition to your business value that you offer, there are a lot of things that affect your website conversion rate, including content structure, copywriting, web performance and interaction design, etc.

Here I focus on my visual and interaction design principles that could increase your website's conversion rate:

1. Use delightful visual storytelling: visual storytelling is one of the powerful ways that can engage your users effectively when done right. Everyone knows a story has three parts: the beginning, the middle and the end. Once you start, you'll tend to learn how the story will end. Storytelling uses that emotion path to guide users through the web content and end up with a call to action.

The left picture shows an example of how visual storytelling compels you to continue scrolling down their pages.

The action that these sites want users to take is to sign up for their emails. Therefore, it starts with a simple but interesting question and then takes users to learn about the answers. The page concludes with a surprising twist ending that creates a great impact on visitors' emotions. That's the right time to offer them a call-to-action item. The same principle is applied for the MARS landing page.

Minh Pham
Vietnam

2. Make your banner a hero: the hero banner is the first thing visitors will see when they enter your website, and they only spend on average five seconds to decide if the site is interesting enough to continue reading. Presenting meaningful animation and interaction at the hero banner will guarantee your audience will place the other foot into your website.

These hero banners below are good examples of this principle: the plane flies away when scrolling down and the island entrance animation strike visitors at first glance and entice them to read more.

3. Use animation to create meaningful UI feedback: feedback communicates the results of any interaction, making it both visible and understandable. UI feedback can be used to reward users after performing an action. The more positively the site reacts to visitors, the longer they will stay and explore for more.

In this example, the visual on the left encourages users to donate more: the more he donates, the better equipped the bear gets.

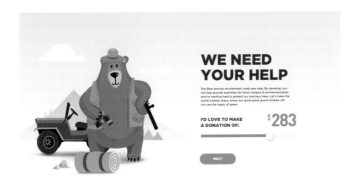

4. Everything leads to the CTA: a CTA is a button or link placed in your website in order to drive prospective customers to become leads by clicking on it and give out their information. Your CTA button has to be the first priority in your site's visual hierarchy. Every visual and interactive element must work together in order to guide visitors to the CTA.

See an example here, the actions are installing the app via App Store or Google Play Store, the two CTA buttons are the most visible elements in this section, the character below supports the CTA by attracting people's attention to him with some simple yet effective animation.

In this example, the visual treatment creates an optical flow that leads your eyes to the center where the core message and CTA stay.

 ## MARS

Designer: Minh Pham

MARS is an app, robot or assistant that guides you through our 30k+ gigantic marketplace of jobs and makes sure you get one really fast. It is designed for speed and uses human-like intelligence to do so. It means that the app can learn, and it is so smart that you can actually have a conversation with it.

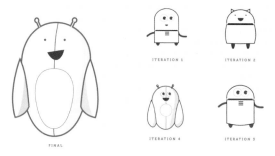

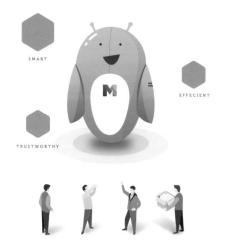

106

LOGO

MARS

ICON

COLORS

 Blue

 Purple

 Pink

TYPEFACE

HEADER
TYPEFACE
Abcd123

Museo

BOLD
ABCDEFGHILKMLNOPQRSTUVWXYZ
abcdefghilkmlnopqrstuvwxyz
1234567890@#$%&^()

BODY
TYPEFACE
Abcd123

Proxima Nova

REGULAR
ABCDEFGHILKMLNOPQRSTUVWXYZ
abcdefghilkmlnopqrstuvwxyz
1234567890@#$%&^()

BOLD
ABCDEFGHILKMLNOPQRSTUVWXYZ
abcdefghilkmlnopqrstuvwxyz
1234567890@#$%&^()

Illustration of a man who is growing in tons of papers or online job posts

What if you have your own job assistant who takes care of seeking the right job for you?

Get started

The problem

Problem 1
Problem 2
Problem 3

Illustrations about the current job seeking problems

The idea

In 2015 MARS started with one smart guy that asked other smart guy asked a question. The question: "If you look at today, how would you have to find a job?"
A group of enthusiasts and a group of large investors shared the same vision. In a few days, one of those enthusiasts used more 200 A4 pages to outline the skeleton of what is now MARS.

Illustrations of the original idea of MARS on sketch paper, showing how MARS connects users with recruiters

The foundation

A large group of bright minds have made MARS. One of the founders has working experience on behalf of Google and managed to capture something of the mystery ingredient which makes their products as good and useful as they are, and applied it to MARS.

Illustration of some men is programing MARS (you can see the robot character is being built)

The Technology

The MARS technology is very special and has never been used before in this way. MARS uses artificial intelligence and machine learning systems which means it is so smart that you can have a conversation with. Our engineers designed it for speed and made easy to use for any age.

Illustration of the character is integrated with multiple skills & knowledge

The product

giant marketplace for jobs where you replace the agency, recruiters or intermediaries by yourself This means that you can have direct contact with the employer and get your job

A smart app that takes care of everything from the moment you start working with your employer MARS arranges everything for your job.

MARS's technology is exceptional Believe us, you can talk to the MARS app as if it's human. You too can do this. Simple.

The Mission

Everyone, young and old can use MARS to get to where they want to be. At this growing rate, in 2019, we'll have 1 million users

We want you to see us as often as possible. In the streets, on TV, in the media and online, and we ask you to be our ambassador. How? Not by selling fried air. But just by showing our app to someone else

Get rid of that agency, recruiters or intermediaries. Do it yourself, use MARS.

1 Download MARS in the Google Play Store for Android or the App Store for iOS

2 Experience and use MARS

3 Have contact with employers and take that job

4 Get Paid

 Available on the App Store
 Google play

MONSTA MOOVE

Designer: Yu-Jia Huang   Country: Taiwan

Monsta Moove is an adventure game that encourages and motives the user to embrace a healthier lifestyle. By reminding you when your body has been idle for too long, litter trainers Moo and Moe will demonstrate workouts that can be accomplished within 30 sec-1 min. Movements appear as fantastical tasks on the screen, such as picking mushrooms, finding treasure in the deep ocean, and flying through the clouds, etc. Each Monsta is designed based on symptoms resulting from an idle body, which includes stressed eyes, weight gain, bad blood circulation, depression, and more. Monstas heal as the user completes missions and moves forward in the game.

1 2 3 4

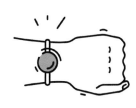

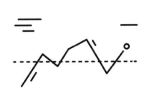

JAPODIAN ECHOES

Designer: Adi Dizdarević   Country: Bosnia and Herzegovina

Japodian Echoes is an audio-visual project based on the rich history of the Japodes (an extinct Balkan tribe). The Japodian story is redesigned for the modern age and enriched by the author's imagination through graphics, visualization and interactive installations.

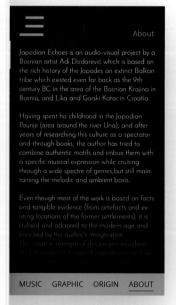

	Year One (2016)			DUA (2016)	+	JE (2016)
	Audio & Graphic			Audio & Graphic		Interactive AV installations

 Metulum
(Year One)

 Purples
(DUA)

 Canyon
Video installation

 Easterns
(Year One)

 Post youth
(DUA)

 Fluo
Sound installation

 Riverine Zion
(Year One)

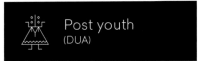 Ocra mons
(DUA)

 Susurri
Sound installation

 Distances
(Year One)

 Pleiades et mons
(DUA)

 Circular reasoning
Generative art / Illustration

 Basma
(Year One)

 Flora 2.0
(Year One)

NEXT-GENERATION USER INTERFACE TECHNOLOGIES

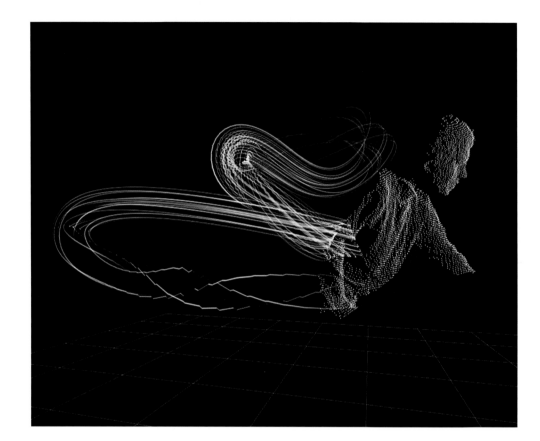

Jean-Christophe Naour
France
Senior Interaction Designer
From Samsung Electronics

In today's world, you must understand interaction design in order to create user experiences that feel fluid and life-like. To connect products to their users through inventive blends of technology and storytelling, interaction design is all about the subtleties.

Design is not solely based on aesthetics or utility, but also the sensation it creates when it is seen or used. Besides, interaction design goes beyond just the visual appearance. It encompasses the ways in which the user will interact with and control an application. If interface design is the look, then interaction design is the feel. Good interactions shape how people interact with individual products. However, great interaction design can shape how people interact with their environment.

My work is often a mix of design and code because I believe that there is something special when the two comes together. Indeed, when I experiment with new graphics and interactions, the rules of computation and algorithm can generate certain patterns and designs in a really special and unique way that I couldn't do by hand. A generative approach allows the possibility to perform ideas as genetic code (algorithm), and to realize, as the natural DNA does, always different and unpredictable series of events, all recognizable by our creative idea. Today the generative approach to art and design represents the best way to carry out the idea as a product, and not only the product as the unique representation of the idea.

Recently we have seen some amazing new technologies entering the scene of interaction design. Just in a few years the technology and interfaces have radically changed and we are moving into an era of highly physical, tangible, and haptic interfaces. All of these technologies are radically expanding the design space. Just a few years back, almost any kind of interaction was all about the screen, keyboard, and mouse interface on a computer. Now, interfaces include questions about what to use (computer, mobile, projected, embed, etc.) and also choices about what kind of interactivity (touch, voice, movements, etc.). Interaction design is apparently not getting easier. The degrees of freedom are increasing, and so is the number of design choices. The only way to deal with these questions is to take it as a multidisciplinary discipline. Interaction design is no longer something that can be approached from just one perspective.

But while we are using several of our senses in everyday life, we are still limited by at most one or two in our digital life. However, **the next interfaces should take full advantage of our complex bodies, which is what multi-modal interaction tends to be.** It should be able to communicate naturally, like using simultaneously the voice, the gestures, or any other method together. But going beyond it demands a new approach, and has crossed the limits of the traditional interfaces (windows, icon, and menu). While the current state of research has not produced robust implementations yet, multi-modal interaction has a big potential.

KINECT GRAFFITI™

Designer: Jean-Christophe Naour

Kinect Graffiti™ is a digital graffiti tool using "Microsoft Kinect" camera. The idea behind this project is to use the Kinect to track the motion behind graffiti by visualizing the body and drawing through different angles in real time, understanding surrounding space, pausing the time, etc. Kinect Graffiti™ tracks the whole body's movement, taking its aesthetic reference from that luminous form of graffiti: light painting.

+ MENU ▼

50 ▓▓▓ LENGTH 28.00 ▓▓ WIDTH 2 SLICES 200 ▓▓▓ SEGMENT

9 ▓▓ TEXTURE 1 TEXTURE_A 1 TEXTURE_R 2 POINTS

POINTCLOUD   SKELETON   PAUSE   LINE   TRACE   CAMERA   RIBBON   WIREFRAME   MOUSE   VCAM

0.00   FRAMECOUNT 10 ▓▓ GRID -2000.00 ▓▓ PCAM

P1   P2   P3   P4   P5

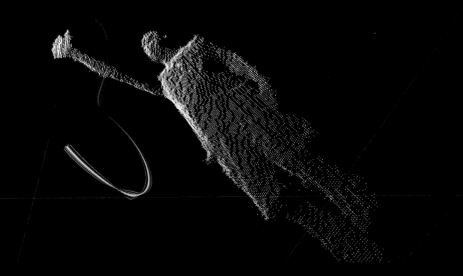

29.876553
MODE : CLOUD

P ▼   M ▼   S1 ▼   S2 ▼

P0   POINT_CLOUD   50 ▓▓ LENGTH   0.50 ▓ FRAMECOUNT

              28.00 ▓▓ WIDTH   10 ▓ GRID

P1   M_MOUSE   2 SLICES   4 POINTS

P2   M_SKELETON   200 ▓▓ SEGMENT   -1400.00 PCAM

                     9 ▓▓ TEXTURE

P3   BOTH   3 ▓ TEXTURE_A

P4   L_TRACE   1 TEXTURE_R

P5   L_BRUSH

INIT L_RIBBON

      L_WIREFRAME

      VCAM

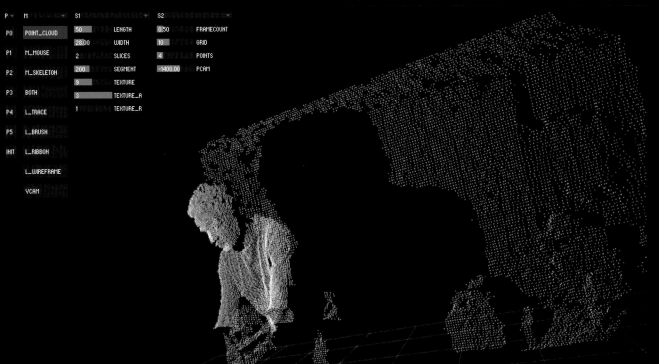

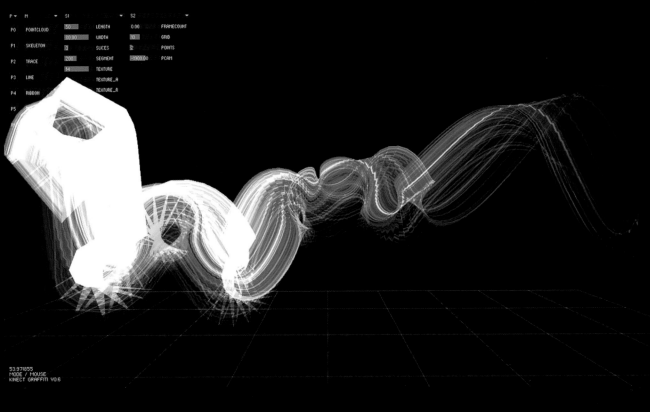

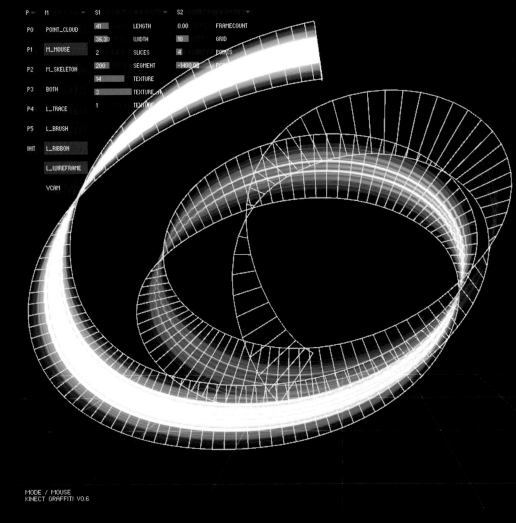

PIXL™

Designer: Jean-Christophe Naour

Pixl™ is a creative tool for iPhone and iPad that lets people to rediscover their pictures. They can play with several settings such as the size of the pixels, the color, the contrast or selecting some patterns. This is a new interactive experience to explore pixels and colors behind photography, and to create countless combinations of fantastic imagery with a simple touch.

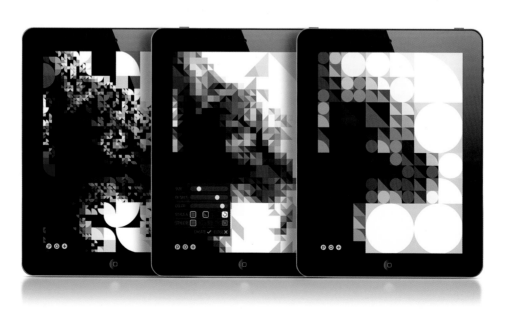

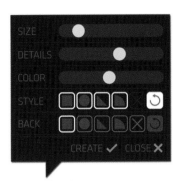
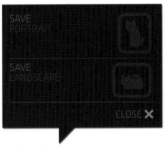

pixl

TAKE A PHOTO

LOAD AN IMAGE

CLOSE ✕

SIZE

DETAILS

COLOR

STYLE

BACK

CREATE ✓ CLOSE ✕

SAVE PORTRAIT

SAVE LANDSCAPE

CLOSE ✕

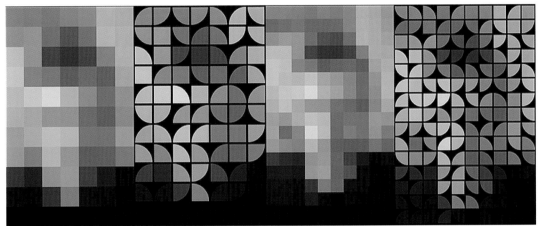

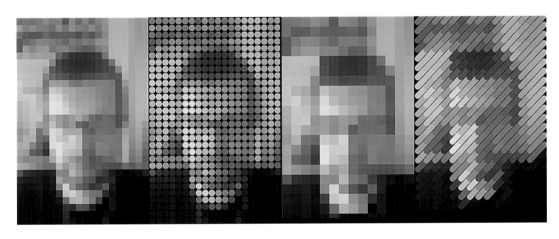

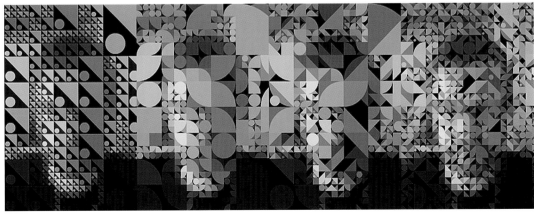

FOODPI

Designer: Mukesh Kumar Ranjan   Country: India

Foodpi is a mobile application which provides the college students across the world the ability to find their favorite restaurants and hotels within or outside the college/university campus. It also provides information about special offers for dinner and birthday party celebrations at a cheaper cost. This application helps to plan a group party with your friends at your favorite restaurants.

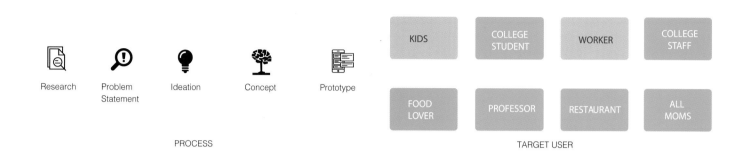

Research	Problem Statement	Ideation	Concept	Prototype

PROCESS

KIDS	COLLEGE STUDENT	WORKER	COLLEGE STAFF
FOOD LOVER	PROFESSOR	RESTAURANT	ALL MOMS

TARGET USER

Location-based Deal

Easy Menu Access

Review

Special Offer

Show Yoor Food

Call

Fast Payment

Book Your Table

Soci Shari

atisfaction

Coupon Redemption

Increase sells

Plan Party

Fast Services

NEED ANALYSIS

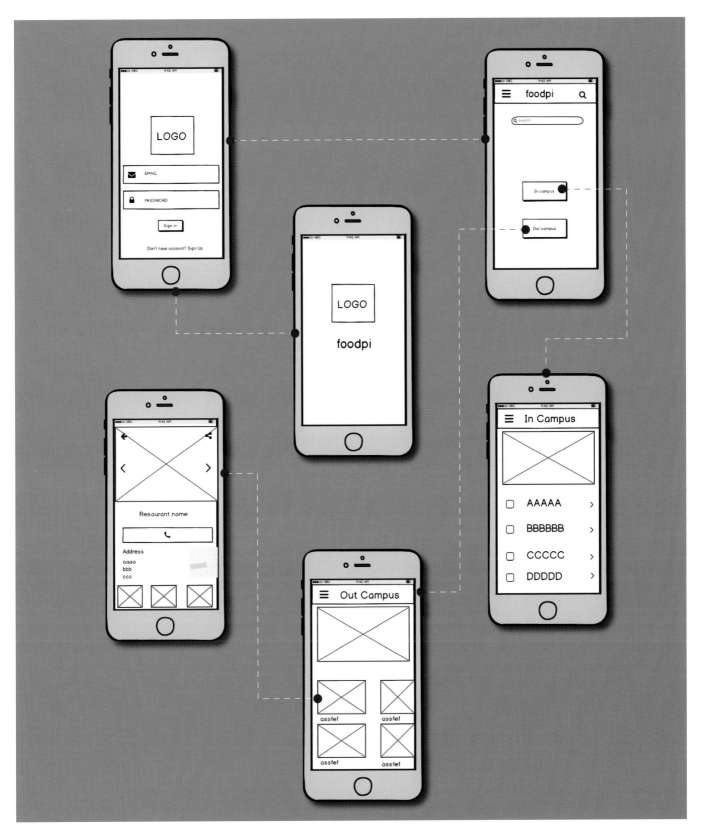

WIREFRAMING

All the user journeys and screen flows were analyzed by generating low fidelity wireframes. Mapping out all the screens states and interactions helped create standardization for the overall user experience and interface design.

Landing Page
The user can search for a food he would like to eat. This screen also consists of an Inside Campus page and Outside Campus page to enjoy delicious food.

Log in & Sign Up

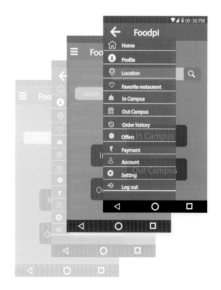

Menu Page
You can save your favorite food & restaurant, change your profile, know your order history, change your location and know best coffee.

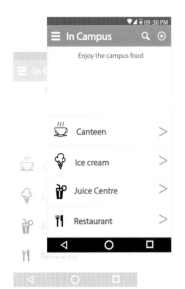

In Campus
The students can search for a food he would like to eat. They can find their favorite canteen, ice cream parlor, juice center and restaurant.

Out Campus
The user can also find their favorite restaurant outside the campus and book their table.

Add Page
The user can also add media, plan parties and add restaurants to database.

Contact Page
Find contact details of restaurants, address and current open or closed status.

ORFEO CONTROL

Designer: Seung-huyn Kang   Country: South Korea

The main features of Orfeo Control include sound effect setting: concert hall, rock, jazz and so on. Users can create a new sound effect by setting an equalizer or 3D sound. In addition, users could hear the sound from outside and check the playing status and function.

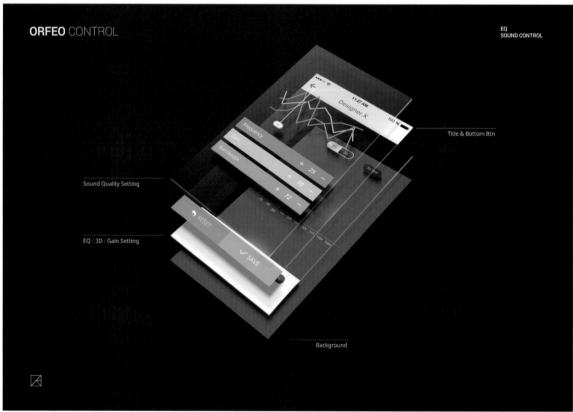

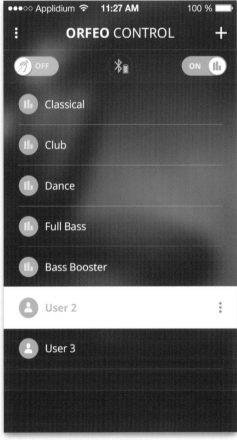

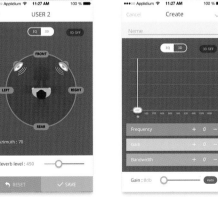

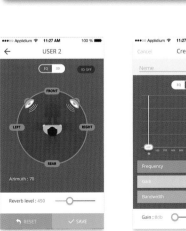

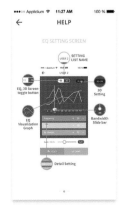

WATCH MASTER

Designer: Seung-huyn Kang   Country: South Korea

Watch Master is an app designed for smart watches. In addition to the basic function such as clock, calendar and weather, it also has new features including health and auxiliary functions. It uses color lump to indicate time, which is eye-catching for teenagers.

Premier Watch
Gear x **Gear**

One by one of the gear is little by little from a predetermined position The time was completed moving Shows

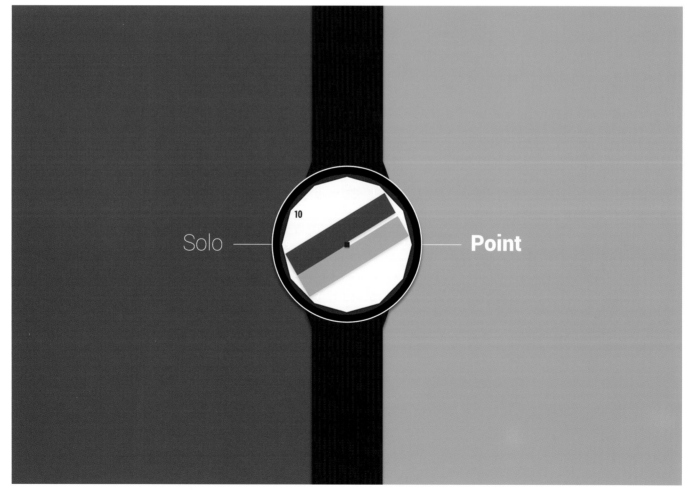

Solo ——————— **Point**

127

MY FACE YOUR FACE

Designer: Seung-huyn Kang   Country: South Korea

"My Face Your Face" is a photo editing app. Users can edit the selected areas of an image and quickly change the look and feel of their images. In addition, the photos can be printed virtually.

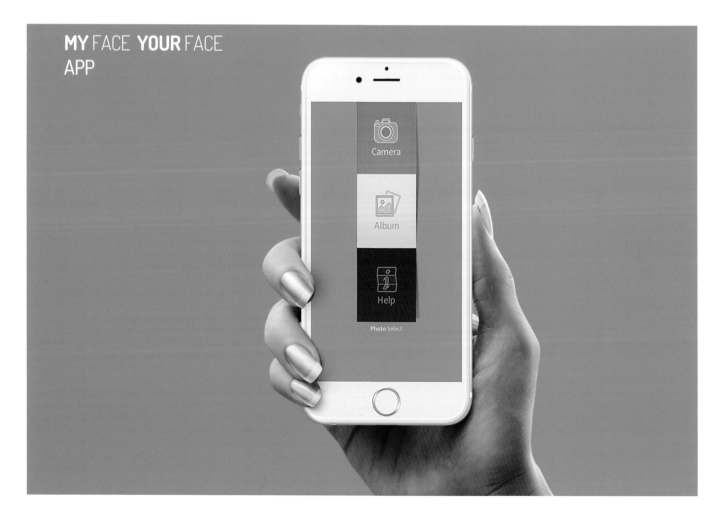

Photo Select Screen
Gender Select Screen
Splash Secreen

Camera Guide Screen
Popup Screen
Control Secreen

Help Screen
Share Screen
Save Secreen

g

GRIDLESS

Designer: Linus Lang   Country: Germany

Gridless is an app which lets the user arrange photos freely. No grid. No limitations. Just stunning compositions.

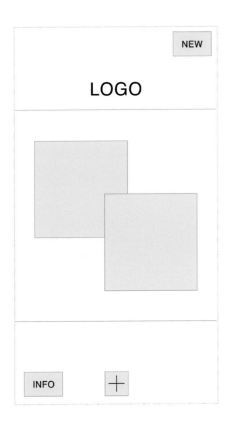

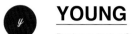

YOUNG

Designer: Isabel Sousa   Country: United Kingdom

In the past, Young was a typical online magazine where teenagers could find the best content focused on their interests. Now, for this always connected generation, Young 2.0 was a new concept where curators use their expertise to make the best stories. The challenge was to rethink an entire brand for this core target market and create a new hub of information for them.

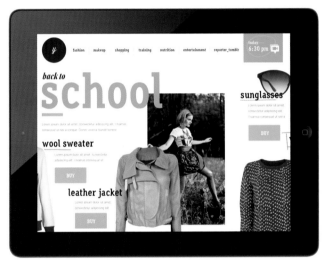

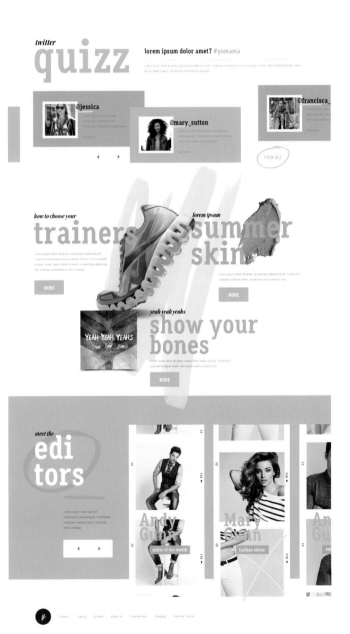

APPLYING PSYCHOLOGICAL KNOWLEDGE TO INTERACTION DESIGN

Laurel Ames
United States

The designer's job is to ensure that all elements of the experience and design are as instinctive as possible. **Identifying and understanding the emotion, action, reward process of habit building is crucial to the development of a successful design.**

When it comes to researching emotional responses, I begin by observing a variety of people interacting in real environments. For example, the research I conducted for my *I'm Hungry!* app began in grocery stores. I studied how people interacted with the space, paying careful attention to where they were looking on the shelves, how they interacted with the products, and their emotional responses in real time.

Once you have a solid understanding of the real world psychological implications of your subject matter, you have to translate it to the digital world. Our business and personal lives are shaped by devices that are designed to collect, inform, educate, and integrate seamlessly. Part of the transition involves applying language and signifiers that people are already familiar with and expanding their meanings to fit this digital context. For example, red signifies danger, warning, or error, while green signifies success or completion. One of the biggest mistakes designers make is leaving context out of the equation. While trends may be cyclical, successful designs constantly shapeshift to the needs of their audiences.

I'M HUNGRY!

Designer: Laurel Ames

Thorough research into brand relationships and neuromarketing has resulted in an application designed to tell the user what he or she should eat based on emotion. The app utilizes the emotion, action, reward system of habit building to simplify the decision-making process while grocery shopping. Interface changes based on the phone's internal clock.

VIMA

Designer: Natalia Magda and Justyna Kusa   Country: United Kingdom

Vima is an app allowing users to create, share and watch premium video content. It is an easy-to-use product that users understand, enjoy and can engage with. The designers crafted each element of user experience, starting from the onboarding process, through search functionality and video recording, to profile area, settings and notifications.

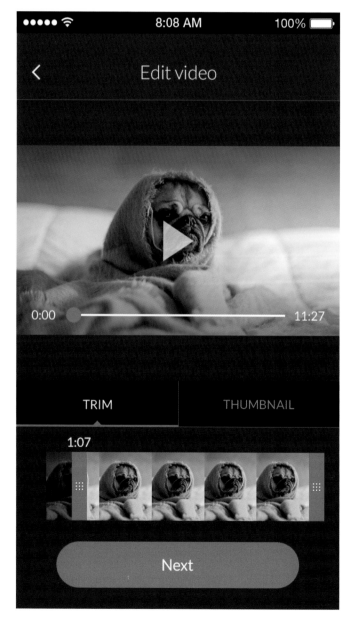

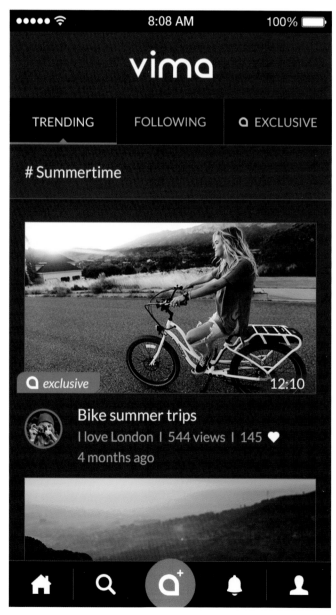

Find thousands of great videos

Explore original TV series, Short Films and Online Content – all in one place.

· · ·

Next

Skip

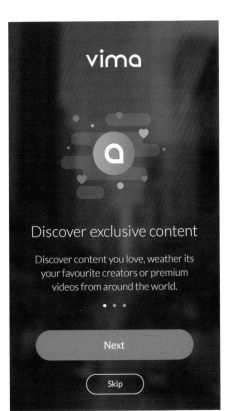

Discover exclusive content

Discover content you love, weather its your favourite creators or premium videos from around the world.

· · ·

Next

Skip

Shoot – Filter – Grow

Connect with likeminded users and grow your own community with similar interests.

· · ·

Got it

exclusive

Watch next
Video Title lorem ipsum et dolor sit amet

FUNCTIONAL

INTERACTION DESIGN

Functional does not necessarily mean plain. The combination of utility and aesthetics is the key to creating the optimal user experience.

SHOPPING

 PHOTOGRAPHY

 FINANCIAL TRANSACTIONS

 BROWSER

HUMAN-MACHINE INTERACTION AND DESIGN THINKING

Joao de Almeida
Portugal

This topic goes through a deep level of human-machine interaction, how we behave socially and thus transmute that into a more intuitive and effective relation with design products.

In general, people's psychological and emotional campus is related to the social need to connect either for communication purposes or status matters. All those emotions must be taken into context because you'll probably have to deal with them in a specific situation for a richer experience.

"Context" is the keyword here. So, adopting an UX/Product design approach will assure us more effectiveness within the experience because, as mobile beings, users/customers live in the "here&now" paradigm. So being able to connect emotionally, staying relevant and respond quickly to a need is our main goal here as designers.

We could focus on psychology, color theory, Gestalt principles and iconology, which are still very relevant nowadays. However, those principles were applied to a narrower sense of interaction, a visual and psychological correlation mostly explored in visual design, or in this case on the web, used for navigation, consistency and usability.

Fortunately, now we have a wider set of senses directly affecting the interaction and thus the experience. There's where human gesture, voice recognition, biometric parameters, among others, take it to a whole different level.

Actually it takes us to the starting point, the human-to-human interaction. This wider set of parameters allows us to assimilate basic human behaviors and transmute them into human-machine relations, resulting in a richer experience with design products and services. So this is not just visual anymore, we have all human senses acting in favor of interaction. Of course those disciplines mentioned above are still crucial for this kind of understanding, for instance, the minimalism approach applied to UI on the web, allows us to get across a more intuitive navigation and focus specifically on the user experience. So we still need those visual principles.

Then, why is this interaction "thing" so important to products, services and business in general? Well, we can now make it more human, more physical, connect things and embed them into our lives. That's how we got to wearable devices at some point. Wearable devices are just a small example of the internet of things, and as a result, human and machine will reach a point where visual disciplines in design will partially shift to product/service design and user/customer experience. That's why interaction design is so important in this transitional period.

ETIHAD: REIMAGINE

Designer: Joao de Almeida

Created by The Barbarian Group and produced by MediaMonks, Reimagined is a five-minute virtual reality film that follows Hollywood superstar Nicole Kidman on a flight from New York to Abu Dhabi. The film showcases the magnificence of Etihad's A380 by taking you on a cinematic tour of the plane. Users can put on the VR headsets and enjoy an extraordinary journey on board the Etihad A380.

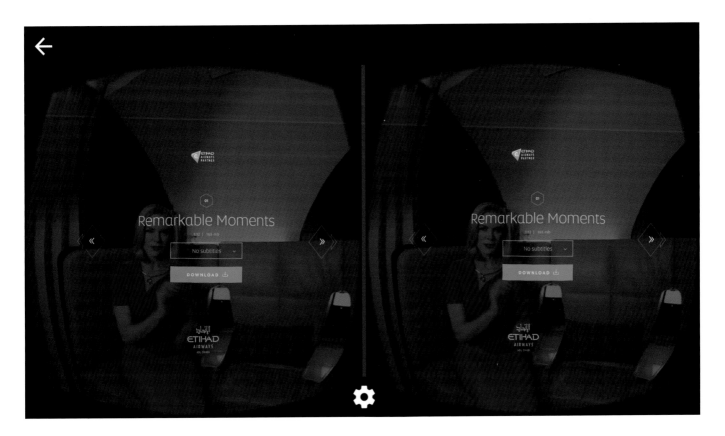

normal

active

 Share

 Share

Icons

Menu normal

Menu active

Timer

HOME

SELECT CARDBOARD / 360 VIDEO

SUBTITLES OPTIONS
CARDBOARD

ETIHAD VR,

Lorem ipsum dolor sit amet, consectetur adipiscing elit. Nulla accumsan dui justo, ac porttitor eros pretium nec.

REMARKABLE MOMENTS

DO YOU HAVE CARDBOARD?

YES   NO

The user can choose cardboard or 360° video.

The background is a 360° image.

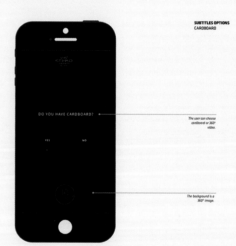

CARDBOARD INSTRUCTIONS
CARDBOARD

CARDBOARD
CARDBOARD

Put on your headphones

Place Phone in Viewer

back

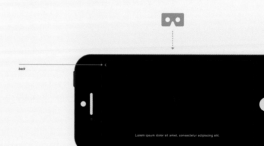

Lorem ipsum dolor sit amet, consectetur adipiscing elit.

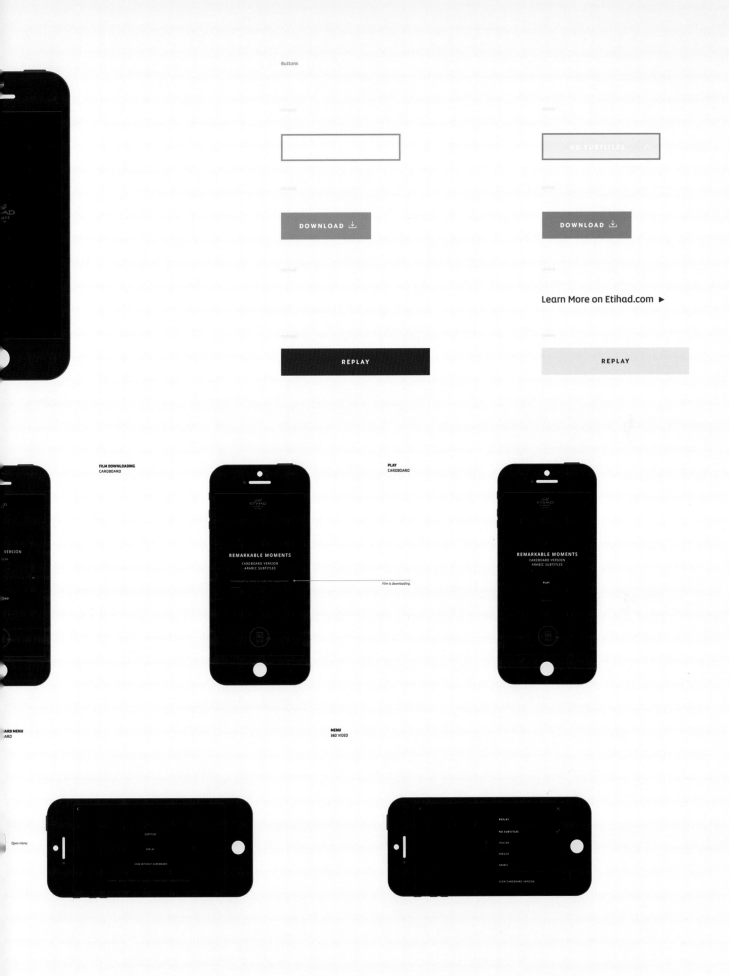

Buttons

DOWNLOAD ⬇

NO SUBTITLES

DOWNLOAD ⬇

Learn More on Etihad.com ▶

REPLAY

REPLAY

FILM DOWNLOADING
CARDBOARD

PLAY
CARDBOARD

REMARKABLE MOMENTS
CARDBOARD VERSION
ARABIC SUBTITLES

REMARKABLE MOMENTS
CARDBOARD VERSION
ARABIC SUBTITLES

PLAY

Film is downloading.

MENU
360 VIDEO

THE GOAL OF INTERACTION DESIGN IS TO PROMOTE COMMUNICATION

10:10:30

12:30:00

14:20:40

20:40:40

Rasam Rostami
Iran
Product Designer

Communication has always been at the core of the design's purpose. Our world runs by infinite relationships between people, objects, environments, etc. And with each member of the system having its own specific qualities, an effective communication is the key to progress. Whether it's a bold red sign saying "WARNING" or a gentle little chamfer on the edge of a smart watch glass, the elements of visual language tend to shape our understanding, deliver the information needed or just match our style.

To create a meaningful and effective communication in this complex and chaotic system, designers try to specify their target group of users, find out what they share as interests, behaviors and needs, then transform and align the visual language elements in a way that makes the perfect match. This is where user interface affects the experience of users. Of course real-life experience of each user differs in innumerable factors from one another, but by analyzing psychological and emotional behaviors, it is possible to make the desired interaction happen.

It is crucial to determine the primary aspect of a design project to decide between trade-offs in the process. For example, if the task is designing a secure login page for an online banking website, after making sure about functionality and minimum failures, designers must take extreme care to deliver the feeling of security. The interaction happens in every element of the interface, a little arrow in front of the login button pointing the page transition direction sends signals to the users by all of its attributes like shape, color, location on the screen and alignment, etc. If the element contains information parameters (like a lock icon for a password field or a badge for a promo code), designers must determine importance level of the message to make enough

contrast. As a rule of thumb, if everything is bold and flashy users cannot find their desired action. Contrast works best when there is obvious different visual weight to the target object.

"It's all about the experience" is something we hear every day. I believe as we go further, experience designers tend to get a more personal approach. **Customization has always been at the core of the user-centered design.** The way each specific user uses an application based on their needs, preferences and interests will (and should) be the main focus in every design project.

3ANGLE

Designer: Rasam Rostami

3ANGLE is a concept sci-fi smart watch face. The idea is about connecting the dots that each pointer is pointing to so you have a triangle on your wrist, constantly and smoothly changing its shape every five seconds.

Settings

Long tap (or force touch) to enter settings menu where you can choose the color scheme or toggle between Day/Night or automatic mode.

EXPENSE NOTE

Designer: Sathish Selladurai   Country: India

This project aims to create an intuitive and convenient application to note expenses of an individual user by involving various scenarios to track the expenditure. And the details will have been added manually by the user.

User Scenario

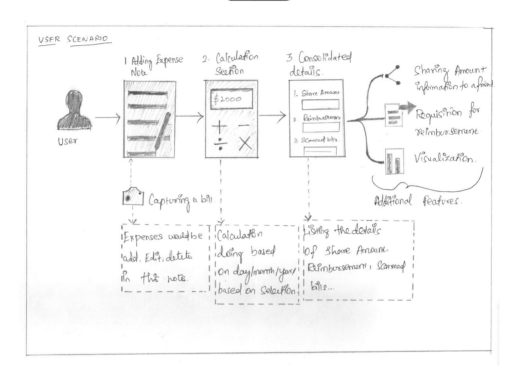

Mind Map

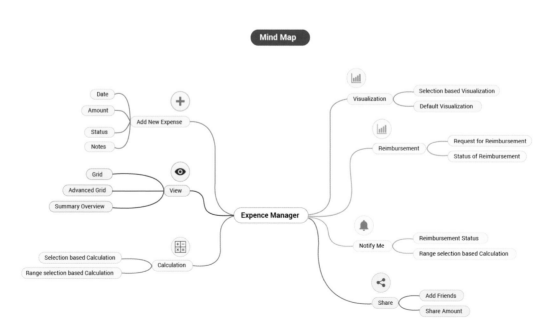

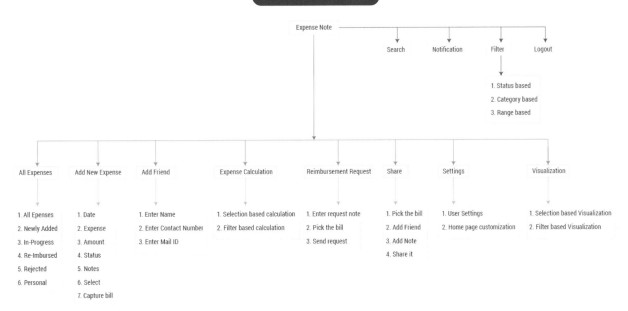

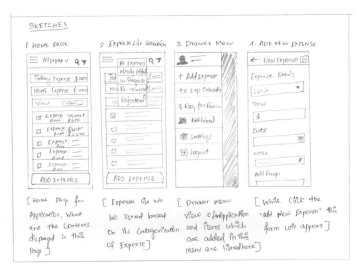

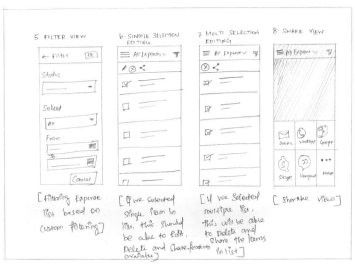

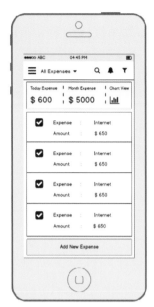

 + = - I chose launcher shape as a Circle since it represents Totality, Wholeness and also denotes a coin shape

Dollar(Currency) symbol   Expense Notes

3
Main Colors

Color Scheme

192 px

144 px

96 px

72 px

48 px

150

1. Drawer Menu

2. Home Page

3. Category Selection

4. Create New Expense

5. Filtering

6. List Expanded View

7. Single Selection Edit Mode

8. Multiple Selection Edit Mode

9. Visualization

10. Sharing Expense

SAFEGUARD

Designer: Karina Popova   Country: Ukraine

Safeguard is an easy and effective method of assistance in these possible situations: cases of stalking, being followed by unknown vehicles, attempted assault, burglaries, kidnapping. That means users can quickly and easily send a signal for help, regardless of location and call possibility. The main function of the application is making the police emergency call without entering the app.

Login Screen
Login screen in application allows the registered user to login to the system or to create an account if he doesn't have it. Users are authenticated against the data stored in the database and once the authentication is successful, users are allowed to log on the system.

Registration Screens
Registration has three fields to enter. Users have to type a new username, password and mobile phone number. After clicking on the continue button, his phone will receive a message with a short confirmation code registration.

First App Screens
After registration, the application offers to user to add the 3 numbers from his mobile in emergency contacts. These contacts will receive a message about your location with a request for help, if you push the SOS button. The police phone number is already included in the default contacts and can't be edited or deleted. The app also recommends to connect your geolocation. If it was not included at the time of signal transmission, the mobile application connects to your geolocation automatically without your confirmation.

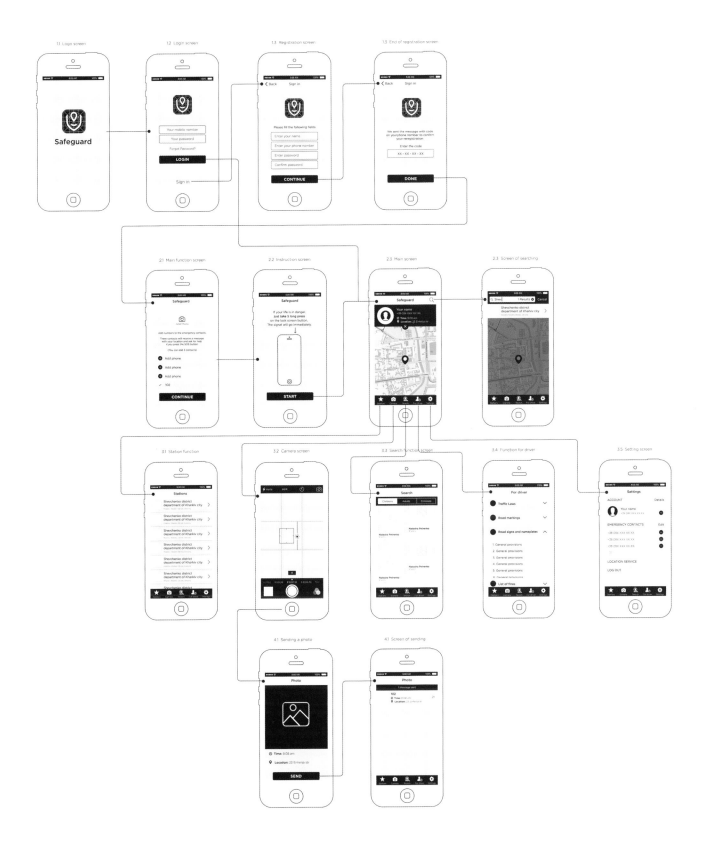

Main Screens
The application will help determine location and provide the closest police station. To do this, on the main screen is a map marked with your location and the exact time and date. Users can see and find any police station in the list.

Sending a Photo to Police
The function of transitions to the camera with the ability to send a photo or video with reference to the coordinates of the location and exact time of the violation or offense.

For Drivers
App constantly updates the information on the recent legislative actions.

Search People
Viewing function of missing persons. Uploaded photos of criminals are separate from photos of missing people and children with their characteristics.

Stations
The list of police stations in the city. The list begins from the closest station to your location at the moment.

Settings
Settings screen consists of the possibility of making changes to the user data, changes in the emergency contacts and exit from application account.

VC BROWSER

Designer: Hongda Jing   Country: China

VC Browser is a fast, secure and smart mobile browser. It offers less memory consumption and more speed when browsing. The app uses purple as the main interface color, which is eye-catching for young people. It adopts the minimum design concept, offering users the ultimate browsing experience.

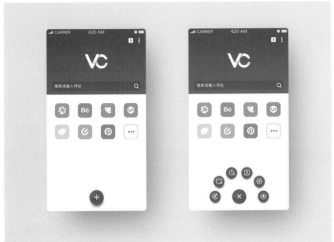

SONG JIANG

Designer：Hongda Jing　　　Country：China

The Song Jiang team is from Tsinghua University. They are committed to making Song Jiang the largest campus transaction platform in China. The designer uses yellow as the main interface color, which looks attractive in the eyes of college students. Users can use the app to look for part-time jobs and online courses.

便捷支付
让支付更爽快

信用消费
我的信用当钱花

无息提现
江湖救急找送姜

V2.1.18

立即体验

SOOJOY

Designer: Hongda Jing   Country: China

This is the VIP version of the Song Jiang app, focusing on good food.

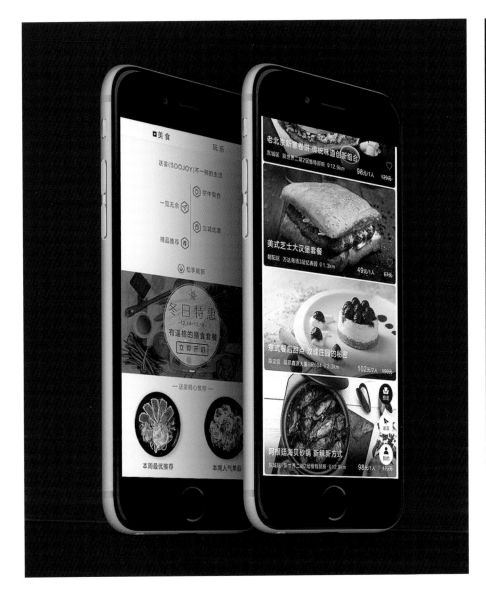

HOW TO DEVELOP A BEAUTIFUL GUI

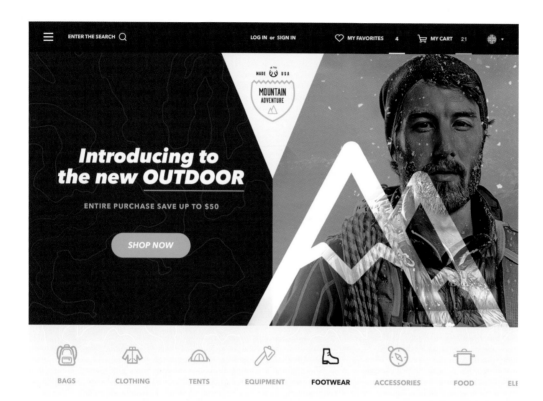

Marcin Mizura
Poland
UI/UX Designer

Unfortunately, the interaction is impossible to evaluate at the conceptual stage. And that is why we have no other options than constant development and testing of the project.

The success of the project may be split into two categories. The first one is connected with sharing exceptional experience and focusing the user's attention for longer. The second one consists in reaching the assumed business targets.

In order to achieve both aims we need to answer two crucial questions: 1.What is the function of the project? 2.How is it going to work?

It will be helpful to get to know more and more about the people who will be using the project. The easiest way to do it is by the development of precise profiles with photos, names and histories of such persons or direct research in a given group of persons. In

the other case, the persons who would be researched should be selected very carefully. We normally apply this method to already existing projects.

Getting to know the people lets us create a project that people will use with pleasure, not because they have to. This is a guarantee that the users will come back to it more often. However, there is a long road to achieve it.

The parts of the project may be visible, audible, touchable or perceivable otherwise, but we must consider the fact that sight is the most important human sense, and we obtain 80-90% of our information by sight.

Every user is individual and perceives colors differently. It is caused by various sight disorders (like the disorder of recognizing colors, commonly called color blindness) and various color settings in the monitor. Most often, we encounter disorders connected with red and green, blue is rare. That is why we should pay a lot of attention to the colors that we apply in the project.

Don Norman wrote that "Nice things work better" in his book *Emotional Design* and this is a perfect example even when designing the wireframe. We should pay a lot of attention to the selection of shapes, pictures, colors and fonts, etc., because it is perceived by the user's subconscious as a complete project. Normally the UX Designer does not really concentrate on this and it leads to various conflicts in the field: UX Designer versus Graphic Designer. One of such conflicts may be designing a different solution for a given part by the Graphic Designer and it may be different than in the wireframe. UX Designers are mostly accustomed to solutions that they already know or have designed themselves and that is why they often destroy the things they do not know.

That is why I believe that in the near future the division between UX Design and Graphic Design will disappear and a merger of both competences will help in developing better and braver projects.

I have noticed that in certain companies such names are no longer used, but are replaced with UI/UX designers or human interface designers. I think it is a good direction, as it combines the competencies, which are mostly the same anyway.

In the future, I expect projects, which, by the combination of the possibilities of sight, touch and hearing, will involve users in getting to know the virtual world. The only barrier is the technology, which is not developed satisfactorily enough at some points of contact.

MOUNTAIN ADVENTURE

Designer: Marcin Mizura

Mountain Adventure has a comprehensive range of rucksacks, walking boots, safety boots, backpacks, sleeping bags, cooking equipment, tents, outdoor clothing, snow boots, camping equipment, running shoes and everything else you could possibly need for an epic adventure.

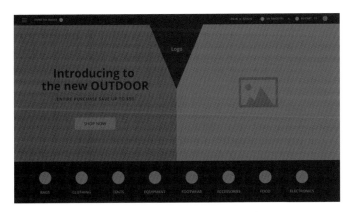

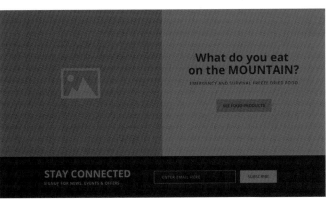

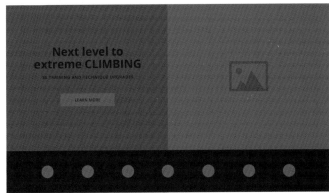

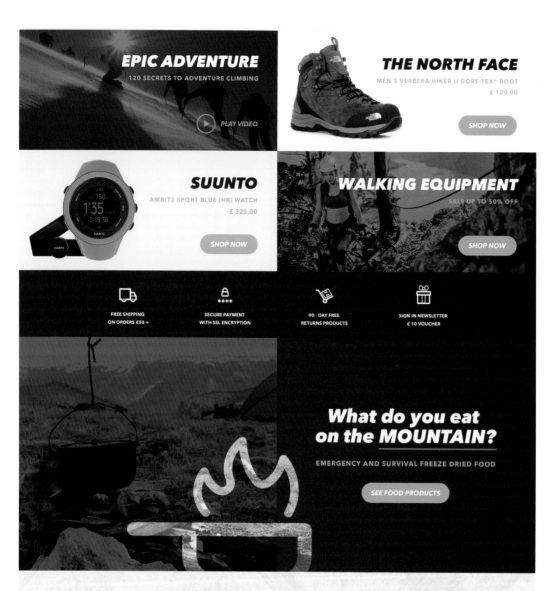

EPIC ADVENTURE
120 SECRETS TO ADVENTURE CLIMBING

▶ PLAY VIDEO

THE NORTH FACE
MEN'S VERBERA HIKER II GORE-TEX® BOOT
£ 120.00

SHOP NOW

SUUNTO
AMBIT3 SPORT BLUE (HR) WATCH
£ 325.00

SHOP NOW

WALKING EQUIPMENT
SALE UP TO 50% OFF

SHOP NOW

FREE SHIPPING
ON ORDERS £50 +

SECURE PAYMENT
WITH SSL ENCRYPTION

90 - DAY FREE
RETURNS PRODUCTS

SIGN IN NEWSLETTER
£ 10 VOUCHER

What do you eat on the MOUNTAIN?
EMERGENCY AND SURVIVAL FREEZE DRIED FOOD

SEE FOOD PRODUCTS

STAY CONNECTED
SIGNUP FOR NEWS, EVENTS & OFFERS

ENTER EMAIL HERE

SUBSCRIBE

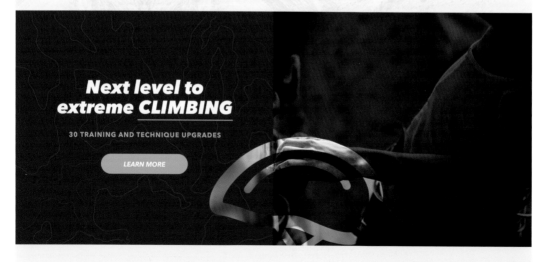

Next level to extreme CLIMBING
30 TRAINING AND TECHNIQUE UPGRADES

LEARN MORE

 salomon MAMMUT SCARPA ◆ Black Diamond patagonia PETZL CAMP

ENTER THE SEARCH

SHOP / MEN'S

PATAGONIA
MR 5 TROUSET JACKET
£ 440.00

BERGHAUS
FRENDO INSULATED JACKETS
£ 440.00

PATAGONIA
MR 5 TORRENTSHELL JACKET
£ 128.00

FJÄLLRÄVEN
KEB LOFT JACKET
£ 195.00

ARC'TERYX
CERES
£ 440.00

SHOP NOW

S   M   L   XL   XXL

ARC'TERYX
BETA AR JACKET
£ 128.00

MOUNTAIN EQUIPMENT
GRYPHON
£ 164.99

FJÄLLRÄVEN
KEB PANTS
£ 440.00

MAMMUT
REALIZATION PANT
£ 128.00

ARC'TERYX
PHASE SV ZIP NECK LS
£ 164.99

THE NORTH FACE
PRISM OPTIMUS DOWN JACKET
£ 440.00

THE NORTH FACE
FREEDOM PANT
£ 128.00

FIND US ON
INSTAGRAM

FIND US ON
FACEBOOK

CUSTOMER SERVICE
CONTACT US
FAQ
PAYMENT
DELIVERY
RETURNS AND EXCHANGES
PRIVACY POLICY

SHOP
GIFT CARDS
HISTORY
CAREERS
TEAM

ACCOUNT MENU
MY ACCOUNT
ORDER TRACKING
WISHLIST
GIFT CERTIFICATIONS

POPULAR STUFF
THE NAPSACK
POLER BAGS
THE TWO MAN TENT
CAMP VIBES COMMUNIQUE
THE LE TENT

HOPPIE

Designer: Amirul Hakim   Country: Indonesia

Hoppie is an application to track employees' satisfaction rate for effective productivity. The main feature is a weekly survey about employees' satisfaction. It also provides a suggestion box where employees could submit critiques and suggestions.

Creative Team

Vinsensiana

Can you make a copy of our last documentation?

10:01

Sure! I'll send it to you by afternoon.

10:01

Orovor

password

Sign In   Sign Up

Question 1 of 5

How happy are you?

35%

0%   100%

⬡ Previous   Skip   Next ▷

💬

Anne Hathaway

Marketing Manager

Question 2 of 5

What is most disturbing you in the office?

◉ Night shift

○ Parking Side

○ Cafetaria

○ Other

⬡ Previous   Skip   Next ▷

💬

Anne Hathaway

Marketing Manager

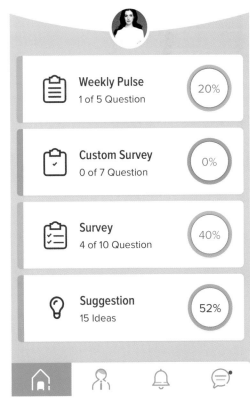

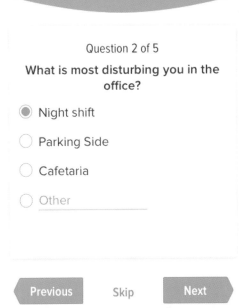

DAY IN 2S

Designer: Victor Berbel   Country: Brazil

DAY IN 2s is a concept app. With the app users can record a 2-second clip every day and stitch them together to make one long clip. The app is easier to use, its name is a representation of the app functionality.

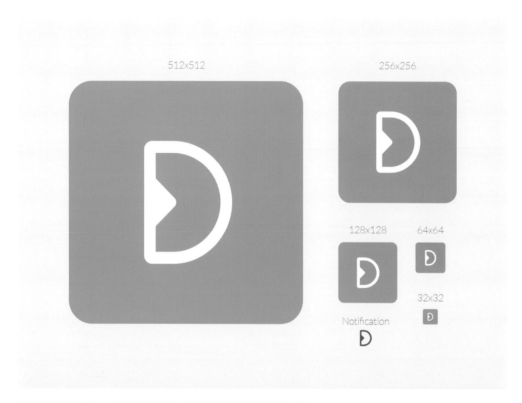

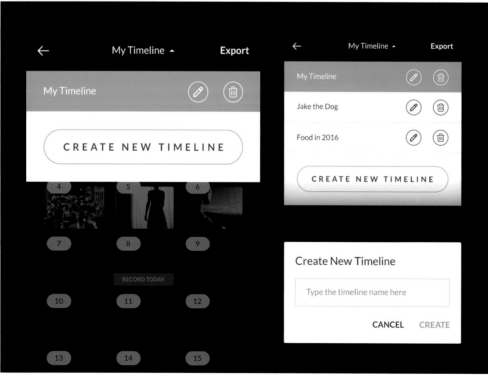

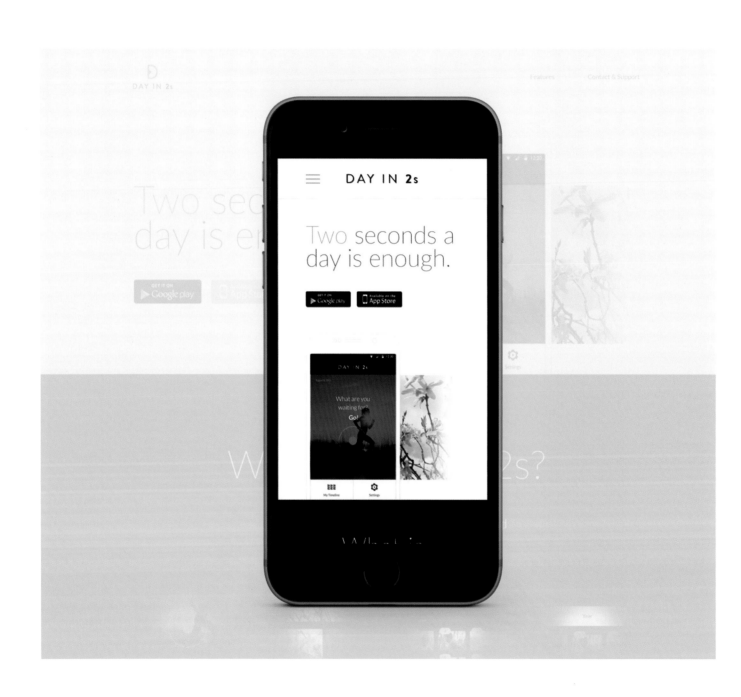

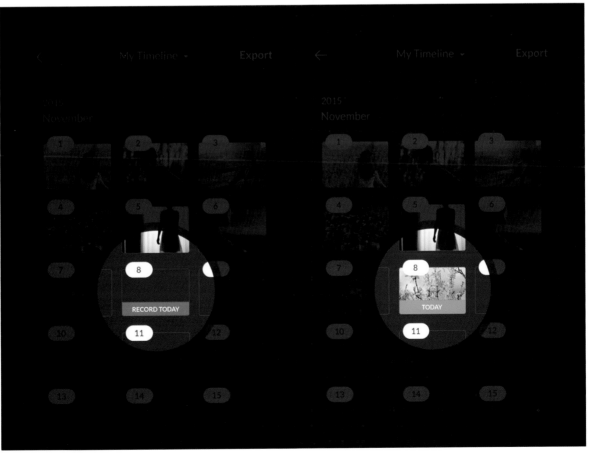

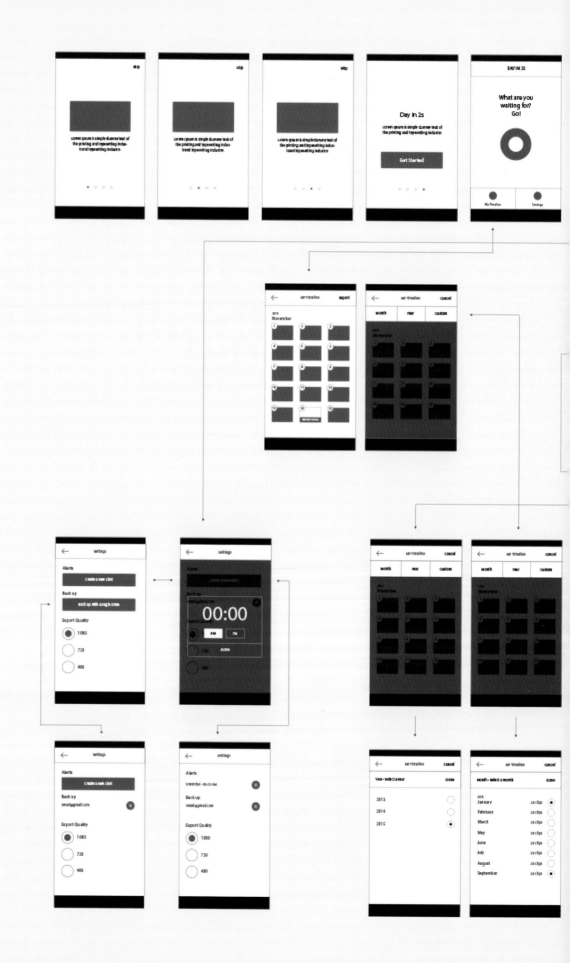

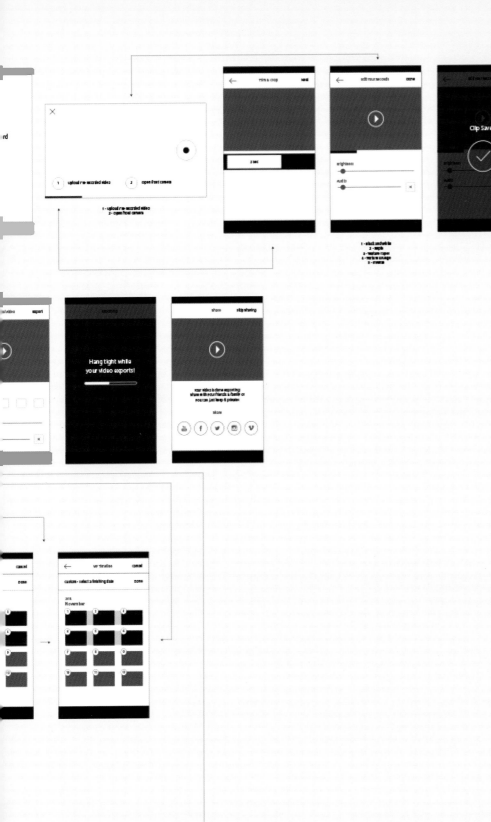

ICBC BANK

Designer：Grace Ge   Country: China

ICBC Bank app offers users a mobile financial services platform with three characteristics. The first is to enrich the function of the product, fully meeting customers' demands for mobile banking. The second is good user experience. The third is a strong safety guarantee, with the industry's leading electronic password and USB key to protect your transaction.

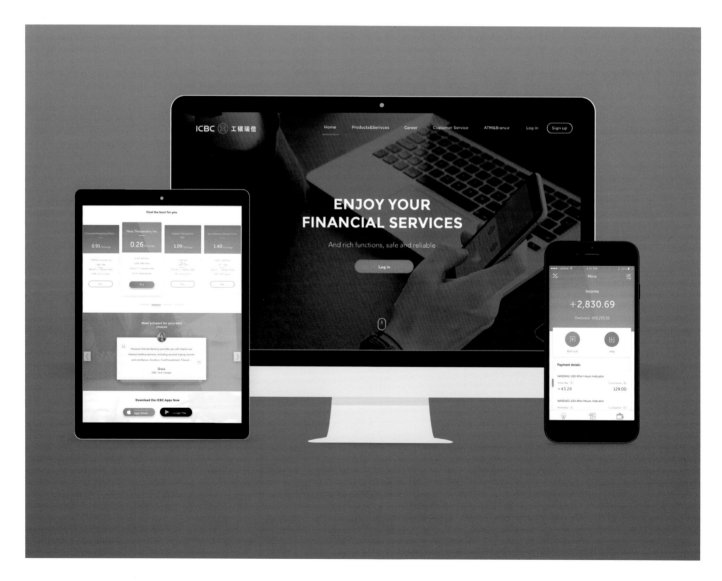

Home

Investment

Mine

Countdown

Price

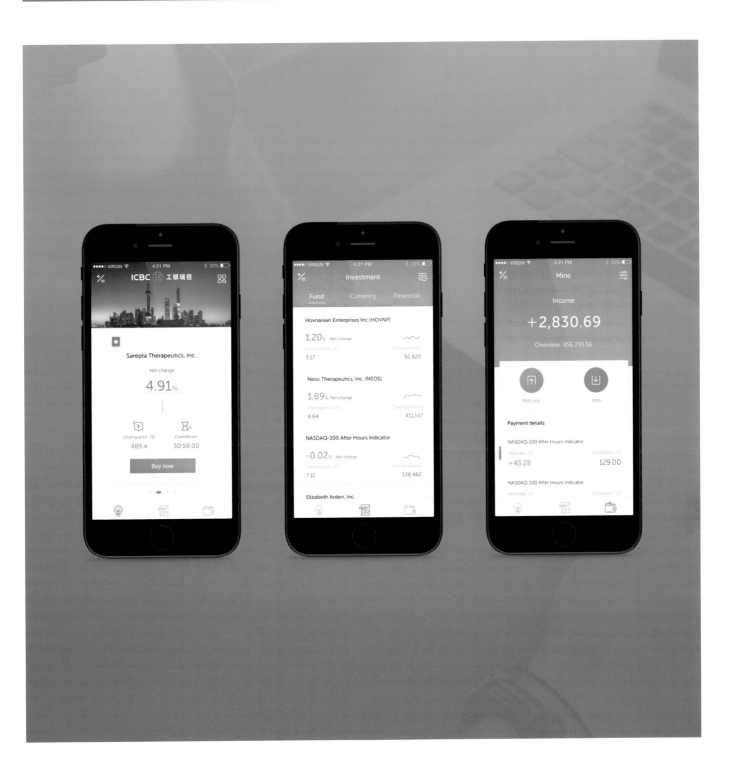

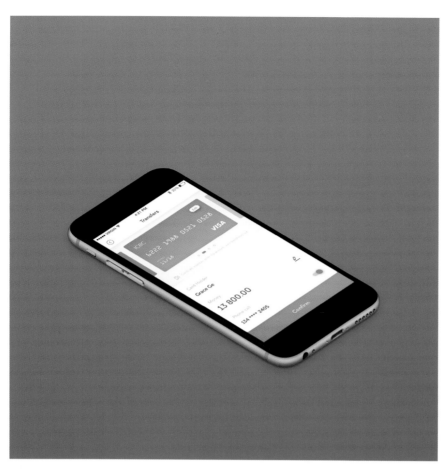

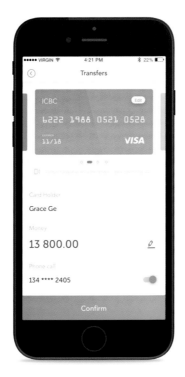

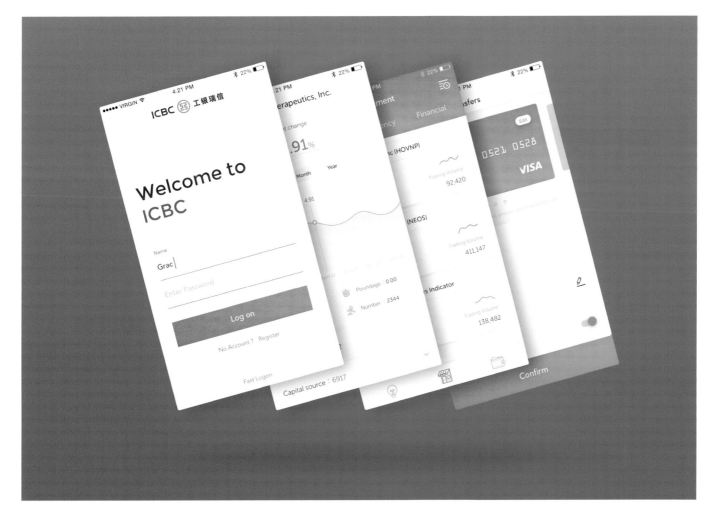

SALES POWER

Designer: Grace Ge   Country: China

Sales Power is a new mobile sales management software, aiming to promote the sales performance of the team.

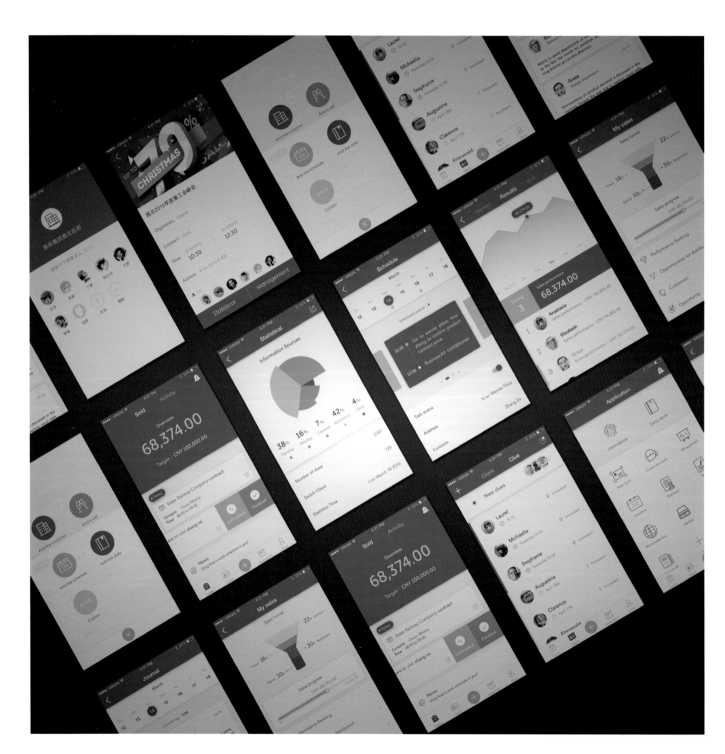

Color

 Main
#4162FF

 Yellow
#FFAF30

 Green
#14B3A2

Grey
#D8DFFF

Icon

 Approval

 Notes

 Announcement

 Scan Card

 Management

 Count off

 Communication

 Data

 Daily work

 Netdisc

PARKMEAPP

Designer: Ceffectz(Pvt)Ltd   Country: Sri Lanka

ParkMeApp is a parking app which allows people to discover available parking spots nearby. It also provides an opportunity for anyone who is interested in becoming the owner of a parking spot. The app gives a comprehensive amount of information about the parking spot and the facilities available, different price ranges based on your vehicle, user reviews, images and street view, including the navigator map, etc.

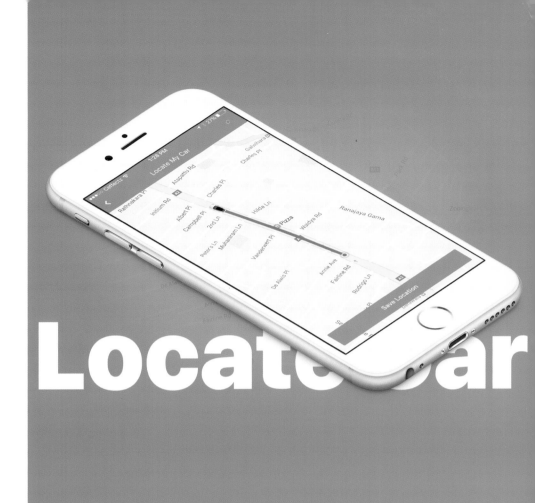

Locate Car

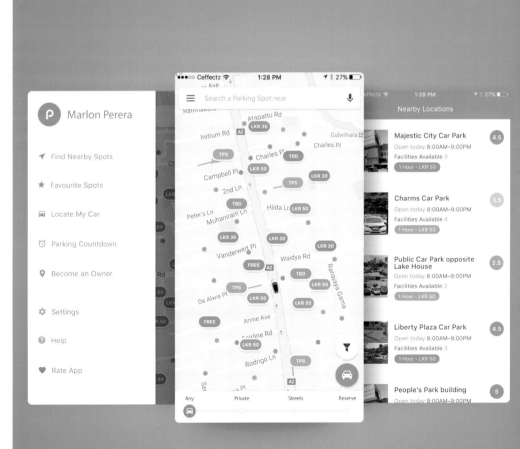

INSPIRATION FROM INTERACTION DESIGN

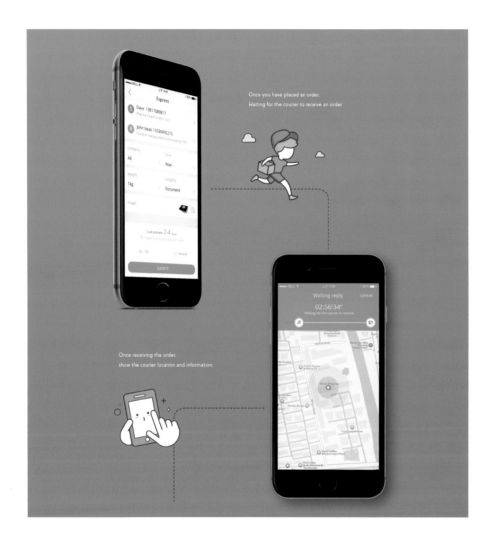

Xiao Zhan
China
UED Director
2017 Silver A' Design Award Winner
2017 K-Design Award Winner

I have been engaged in the interaction and visual design field for over seven years. People usually ask me questions such as: "Are there any principles in interaction design?" "How do I enhance the user experience?" I was not able to provide a detailed answer that time. Therefore, I want to take this opportunity to talk about the classical principles of interaction design in detail based on my own experience and understanding.

Visibility

The function of a product should have enough visibility that the uses can clearly know what the next step is. If the function is too difficult to locate, then users will seldom use the function. To put it simply, the designers should highlight the core features by using certain colors and icons and hide the secondary functions. This interaction design method is called "subtraction", which is very difficult to do. The designers should understand users' demands and control the operating area of tasks, so as to let users use the product in an easy way. For example, "Wechat" app puts the main function such as "scan" and "add friends" in the upper right area. Therefore, users will have a strong impression toward the main function.

Natural Mapping

Simply put, the function of a product should be "natural" and conform to human nature, so that users can easily get started without word descriptions. For example, my four-year-old nephew found it easy to use an iPad. The unlock feature of the iPad is easy to use without learning. The reason is that touch and psychological suggestion is human nature. Therefore, good interaction should conform to human nature.

Consistency

The structure, interface, style and control of a product should be highly consistent. For example, iOS has iOS Human Interface Guidelines and Android has a Material Design Principle. They set detail design specifications so that products have high consistency. On the contrary, if the home buttons of the iPhone, iPad and iTouch are triangles, rectangles and none respectively, would you still love Apple products?

Cognition

If users have a clear understanding of the function, then they better know how to use it. When we are doing design, we should base it on users' psychological models rather than a logical, authentic and accurate model. Those interfaces are usually not effective and difficult for users to understand. Most users don't care about how to run a program. For example, when the audience is watching a high-speed video film and marveling at some details, they do now know the high-speed video films could record at a speed of 1000~10000 frames per second. Therefore, the designers should build the core user scenario based on users' psychological model.

Emotional Design

As far as I am concerned, the emotional design is a "considerate" design, paying attention to users' goals and needs. Emotional design does not mean satisfying users' needs blindly. There should be a boundary. User experiences should be designed according to different emotions. For example, we all played the game "Super Mario" when we were young. Every time when we pass a level, we do not need to control the game, instead we watch the game video play automatically, which allow users a moment to relax from the nervous and exciting game experience. Another example, I went to Japan two years ago. I found that the paper core in my hotel toilet is actually quadrangle. Therefore, it is less convenient to pull the paper down comparing to a round paper core. The design aims to convey the idea of saving resources, which is a good combination of business value and user emotion. In short, the designers should study and experience user's emotions as best as they can.

Error Control

When designing a system, try your best to avoid users making big mistakes. However, few products could be able to do this. If users make a mistake, the system should indicate the cause and provide simple and intelligible solutions to deal with the mistake, rather than leaving users on the error page. For example, both Word and Photoshop provide an "undo" feature; can you imagine using them without an "undo" function?

Brand Impression

Defining brand temperament. The "temperament" includes the design style, aesthetic, culture and spirit of the product design. Designers should think and verify the elements and come up with a unique brand temperament. The objective is to let readers identify your brand and eventually fall in love with your brand culture. Speaking of simplicity, technology and user-friendliness, you may think of Apple, and that is the so-called impression of a brand.

Business Value

Design is different from art, where design is rational and has methodologies. A good design will enable users to achieve their goals and be more efficient. For example, the first automobile was a three-wheeled motor car, which looks quite odd. Later, automobiles with easy operation and good looks have been developed, which means designers added business value to them. In the past, design may mean product, project and solution. Now, design is more of a mode of thinking. The combination of design and technology enhances new business values.

ATXIAOGE EXPRESS DESIGN. CLINET VERSIONM

| TYPE | CLINET | DATE | SERVICE |
| iOS App | ATXIAOGE | Fed 2016 | UXIUI |

ATXIAOGE

Designer: Xiao Zhan

ATXIAOGE platform is an O2O app based on LBS, mainly serving C-terminal customers who have a shipping demand. Users could load their demands on the app, and the courier mode will display the needs so that the delivery person could receive the order.

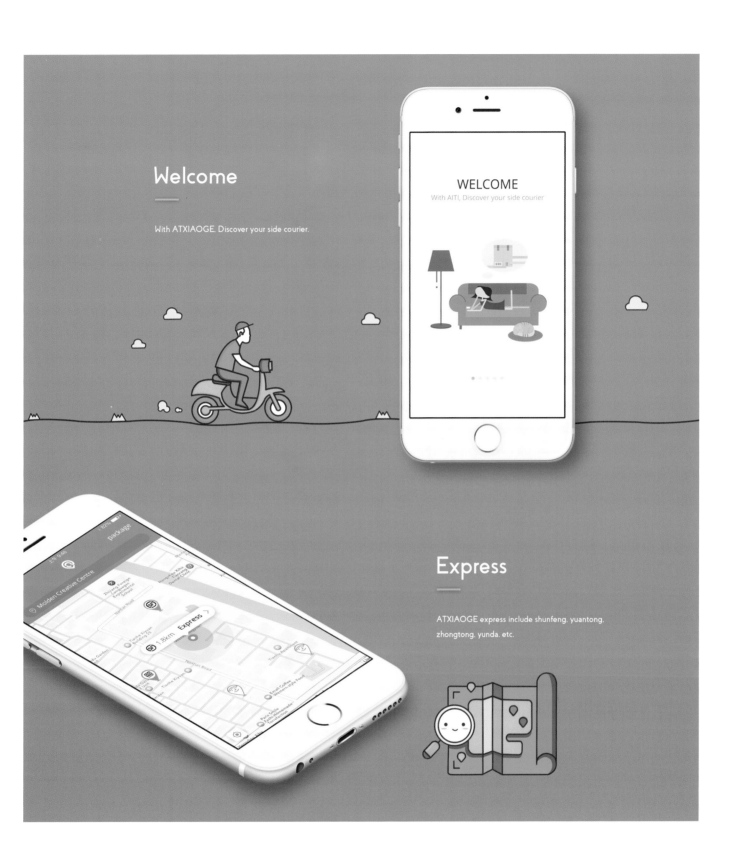

Welcome

With ATXIAOGE. Discover your side courier.

WELCOME
With AITI, Discover your side courier

Express

ATXIAOGE express include shunfeng. yuantong. zhongtong. yunda. etc.

FQGJ

Designer: Xiao Zhan

FQGJ is a bill management tool designed for the young generation. It helps users keep a sound credit record by providing smart repayment alerts and emergency repayment channels. Combining hundreds of online installment and loan platforms, it provides smart loan searching services, greatly enhancing the success rate of obtaining a loan.

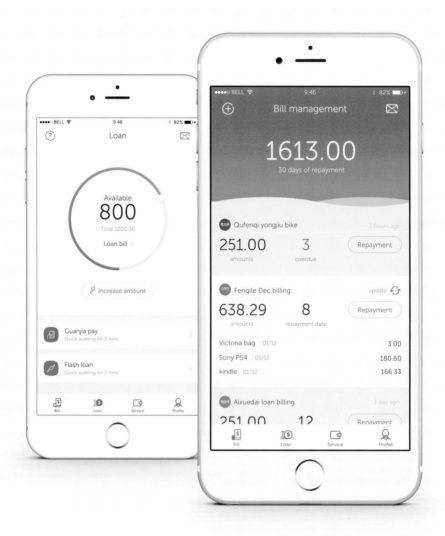

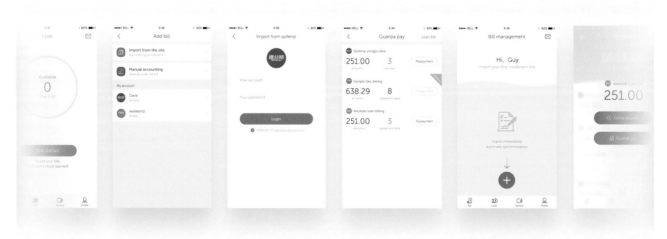

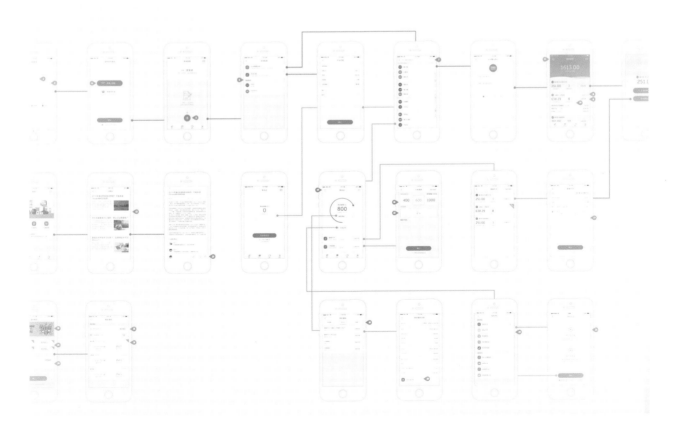

TOUR IN HANGZHOU, ROAM AROUND WEST LAKE

Instructor: Xuefeng Bi   Design team: Aoshen Guo, Junzheng Guo, Yu Zhang   Country: China

The project is a conceptual design combined with sightseeing interaction and media to present ten scenic spots and history-related information of the West Lake to visitors by popular interactive means. It is explored as a brand planning based on the resource of West Lake and a system of memorable action in the trip with an aim to promote the development of the tourist spot. Meanwhile, a series of derivatives of West Lake are developed by this theme.

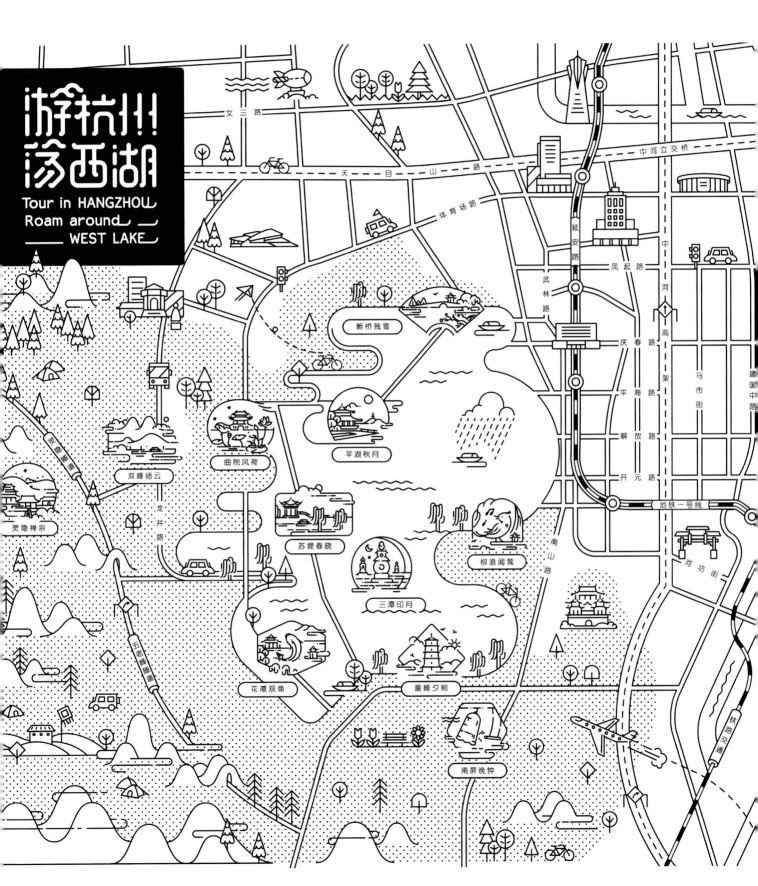

游杭州西湖

Tour in HANGZHOU
Roam around
WEST LAKE

文三路

中河立交桥

天目山路

体育场路

延安路

凤起路

武林路

中河高架

马市街

建国中路

断桥残雪

庆春路

平海路

解放路

开元路

灵隐飞来峰

曲院风荷

平湖秋月

双峰插云

龙井路

灵隐禅宗

苏堤春晓

柳浪闻莺

南山路

地铁一号线

河坊街

三潭印月

五老峰隧道

花港观鱼

雷峰夕照

南屏晚钟

铁路交通

GREAT UI IS INTUITIVE AND INVISIBLE

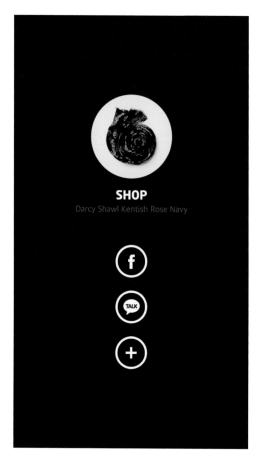

PlusX
South Korea

Interaction design is providing a brand, product, and story with an intuitive and interesting look to users. 29CM is not a space that simply buys and sells goods but a space to share the brand's values and emotions. Therefore, the functional side is important. But above all, we tried to put emotional things into the service.

In terms of design, the optimized design for mobile devices is realized by minimizing color/line/surface and reducing the complexity to increase the concentration of the content. If interaction elements were used excessively, information communicability may fall. So we excluded excessive interaction and added details to small elements like 'Heart' and 'Share'.

The motif of "heart flutters" was used as a select function. Generally, the "share" button exposes in screen. However, this button is hid in 29CM and users can split the screen anytime and anywhere by the gesture of Pinch In/Out and the "Share" button will appear. In the list screen, the tedium of repeating long scrolls was reduced and the "Following Text" function was added to give some fun to users. Besides, interactions are applied in the service of using coupons, putting products in a shopping bag and activating the search bar, etc.

In conclusion, we think commune with variety of interaction through the natural finger gesture is 29CM's advantage. If communication is an expression language between man and man, then a gesture has to be one of the means of communication between devices and people. **In the future, how to access the third screen easily by large and small gestures will be a main task in terms of interaction design.**

29CM

Design: PlusX

29CM is a shopping platform that tells value of the brand and product to help customers to make better choice. With a simple and beautiful user interface, this app allows users to shop anytime and anywhere. It highlights the characteristics of the product display so that customers have a better consumer experience.

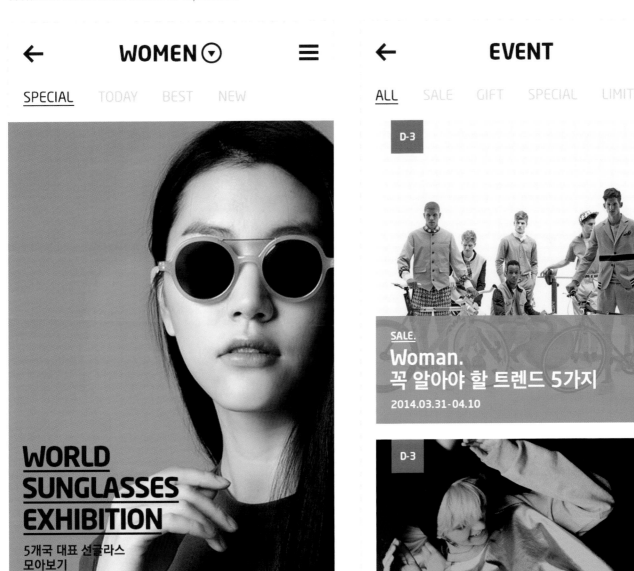

Pomegranate Diffuser
애프터아워 스튜디오 석류 디퓨져

SALE

HUBERD'S SHOE OIL

~~2,000won~~
20% 1,600won

영국을 넘어 전세계 130개의 샵으로
확장됩니다.

← PT ⓘ ≡

HISTORY   **NOW**   COMING

ING

몰튼
09:57:20

29CM COUPON

20%

몰튼 자전거 스페셜 구성
20% 할인
2014.03.24 - 2014.04.07

↓

SHOPPING BAG

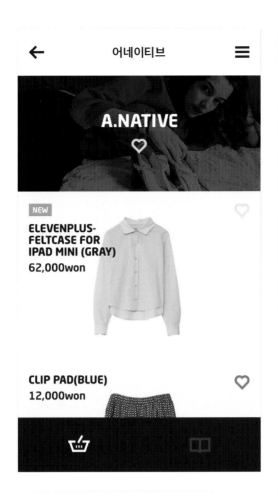

← 어네이티브 ≡

A.NATIVE

NEW

**ELEVENPLUS-
FELTCASE FOR
IPAD MINI (GRAY)**
62,000won

CLIP PAD(BLUE)
12,000won

← SEARCH ≡

릴라바이로타 🔍

FOR THE DAY

—

불금엔 이렇게

오늘은 튀면 안돼

회사 갈 땐

결혼식엔 이 느낌으로

시크하고 싶은 날

⊕

← Collection 31 : 끝이라는... ≡

D-3

KINFOLK

🔍　　🛍️⁸　　♡

29CM HOME

**WOMEN
MEN
HOME
LIFE STYLE
CULTURE**

**SPECIAL ORDER
PT**ING
BRAND

WHAT MAKES A GOOD UI

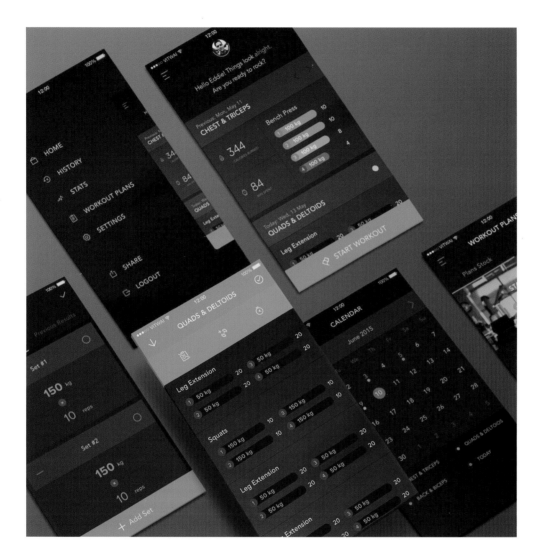

Vitaly Rubtsov
Ukraine
UI/UX Designer

So far, communication between people and machines possesses machine character. Despite the development of human-centered computing, a person is still forced to think in a way he or she is not used to and to adapt to the machine logic. A programmer's attempts to describe the details of software implementation to the system trigger different restrictions and algorithms that are unusual for a human logic. There is even a notion called "computer literacy" which Alan Cooper mentioned in his books.

There is no need for a user, though, to know the details of software implementation and even more so to adapt to computer logic. A machine needs to adapt to the needs and wants of a person, not vice versa. We do not think how a smartphone functions while using an app, or how a projector in the cinema provides a picture on a big screen while watching a movie. What we do have is a general idea of how we should use this or that mechanism, or something called a "mental model."

Working with a "mental model" is one of the main aspects of a designer's job. It requires putting aside the "implementation model" all together, and concentrating on simplicity and convenience of use instead.

In the past couple of years, we have seen a mass movement to combat the "implementation model" by promoting ease of machine use to the dominant positions. Given the rapid spread of programs, websites and apps, there appear to be more and more user interfaces ready to transform our lives by offering better user experiences. All this technology is so tightly integrated into our everyday life that it becomes mundane. And there is nothing wrong with that. After all, user interfaces and technology as a whole are just tools for doing things and achieving goals.

When it comes to smartphones, the ease of use becomes even more crucial. Nobody will read manuals or watch video lessons to learn to use a mobile app. **Therefore, designers need to put all their efforts into making an intuitive user interface without explanation.**

WORKOUT BOOK

Designer: Vitaly Rubtsov

Workout Book is a workout tracking app concept. The interface is simple and easy to start for new users.

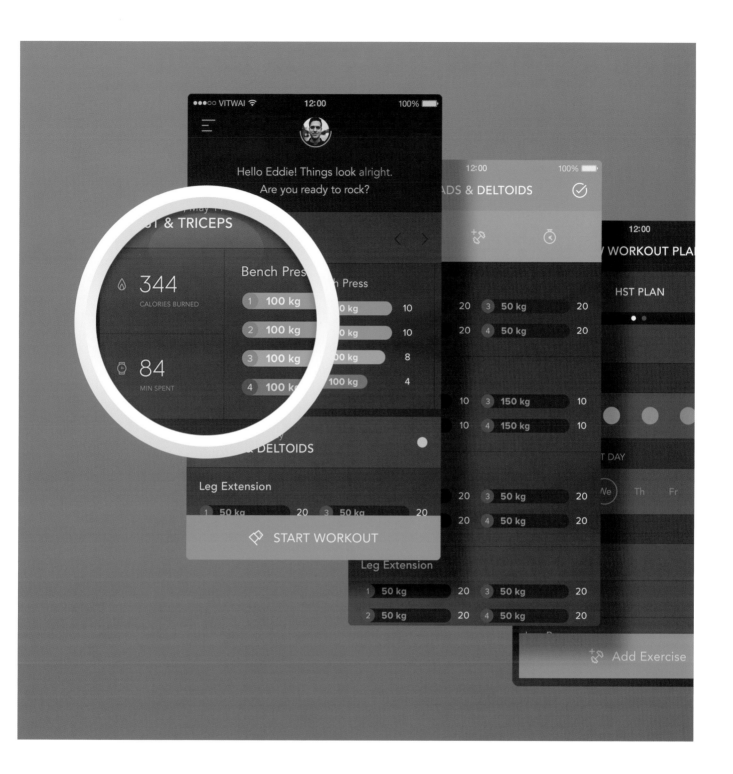

THE KEY OF INTERACTION DESIGN

Tong Wen
United States

The relationship between interaction design and people is like love. When they first meet, design should be attractive so that people fall in love with design. After living together, design should listen, understand, and fulfill what people need. In other words, interaction design is not always user-centered but also design-centered. Mutual equality is the key to a better love.

The most typical media connecting people and machine is interface. On an interface, the main elements can be roughly divided into "VACANCY" and "INFORMATION". Vacancy is both solid and not. As solid, VACANCY plays a role as container wrapping the information at the same level. When VACANCY is gaseous, it separates information at different levels. All in all, VACANCY is the most crucial element for building info hierarchies.

Regarding "INFORMATION", the visual approach applied to information must be reasonable, and meeting certain functional needs. Color, shape, size are supposed to be considered properly so that the INFORMATION talks about itself effectively and efficiently.

Building a structure (or design guidelines) to which all the elements can apply is the key of interface design. In this way, the design outcome follows simplicity rule, since design decisions at different scales all depend on only one structure.

Richness is also achieved at the same time. It is just like the natural phenomenon "FRACTAL". Fractal can be nearly the same at every scale. This simple rule comes out of the complex and varied pattern.

There is no limitation in interaction design. Once ago it was defined as interactive activity between machine and human. But actually, it could be mutual effect among anything anywhere and anytime. In other words, "No limitation" is substantially the biggest limitation of interaction design. Only by defining the right constraints and designing beyond the limit can interaction design evolve into a more critical and insightful design field.

ME.TRAVEL

Designer: Tong Wen

When people begin to organize a trip, the first thing they do is find something interesting in the city, then build up a plan to visit. Existing apps had sightseeing data and information, but no way to make a schedule of what to see and when - there was no way to connect those two things. The designer wanted to link the two in a single place, with an easy interface.

FITBARK

Designer: Michael Chiang Country: United States

The designers are on a mission to get dogs and humans healthy together. A dog is an ideal exercise partner, and being commited to a dog enables us to commit to physical activity ourselves. So they designed FitBark, a beautiful sensor that monitors your dog's daily activity and sleep and turns it into BarkPoints, so you can track progress. It's a new way to keep your dog (and you!) healthy, explain changes in behavior, make better decisions with your vet, and share memorable moments with friends & family.

IFEEL - MOOD TRACKER

Designer: Nhan T. Hoang   Country: Vietnam

It's really important for people who use a mood tracker to see how their moods go during the day or week, because life is not easy, there are always ups and downs, and there is not a single moment in one's life that could be considered the end of the world, it always gets better. Failures, sadness or depression, they are quite normal things in life. The designer wants people to look at the graph in the app to see that—once the moods go down, they will go up after.

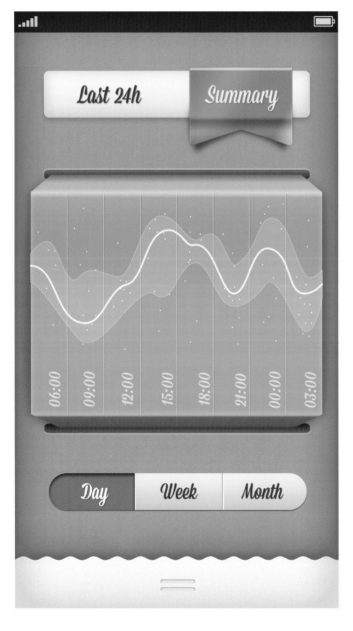

How are you feeling?

How are you feeling?

Excited!

How are you feeling?

Satisfied

How are you feeling?

Blah...

Sign Up

Pick a Username

• • • • •

Create an account

By signing up, you agree with this
Terms of Service & Private Pricacy

Settings

Simonhoang   Sign out

Sync data to server ⊘

Also post on Facebook ⊘

° UI AND BRAND EXPERIENCE

Igor Savelev
Russia
UI/UX Designer

User interface and interaction has become an important part of the brand experience for traditional offline companies and especially for online business. It is the place where the user touches the brand. Through the style, attention to details and micro animation, we can create a correct experience of a brand by the user. We should help interfaces to respond better to user actions. Globally, it is just a modern language between human and machine, users and service, brand and customers.

Interaction design must manage user's emotions. For sure, it should convey positive emotions while avoiding negative ones and it is critical to product success. The usage of dynamic icons, animations and sound, font combinations and color palettes can help to create an interactive interface, to get feedback, to influence users depending on goals that brand or product wants to achieve, all that can affect a user's perception of usability.

In the nearest future, this approach will become especially important as companies put their focus on communication with the user only through the digital interfaces.

FAMILIES

Designer: Igor Savelev

It is hard to remember all the events of wedding anniversaries or birthdays of children. With this app, users no longer need to keep dozens of reminders, alarms and notes. It is easy to track all family events, anniversaries of family members and friends in this app.

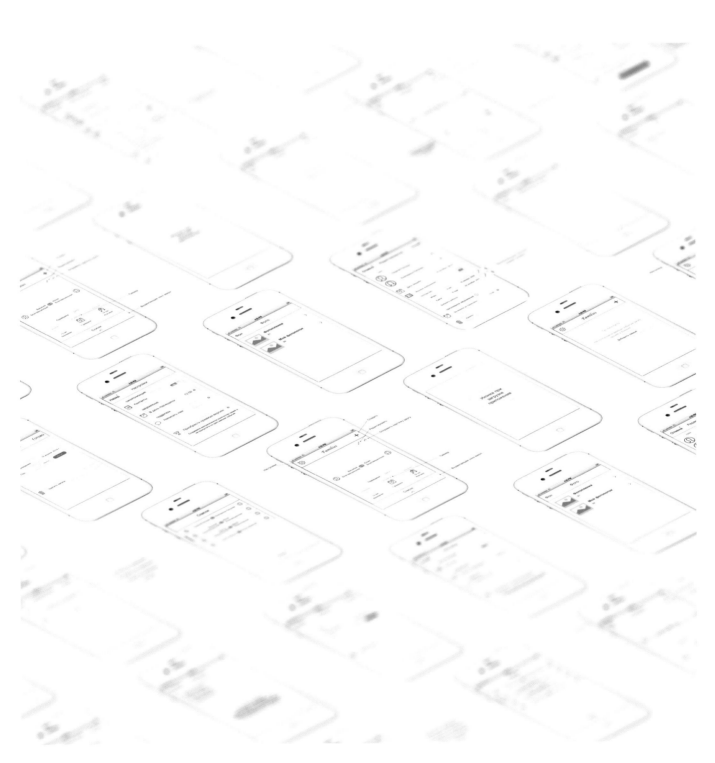

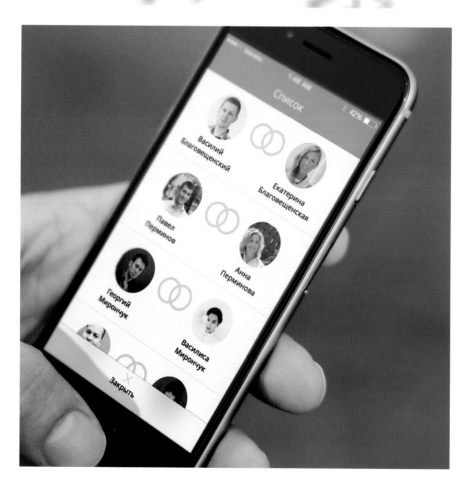

HUGE IOS UI PACK

Designer: Igor Savelev

This app allow users to create their app design, prototype or get inspired with more than 200 iOS screens and hundreds of UI elements, organized into 8 popular content categories.

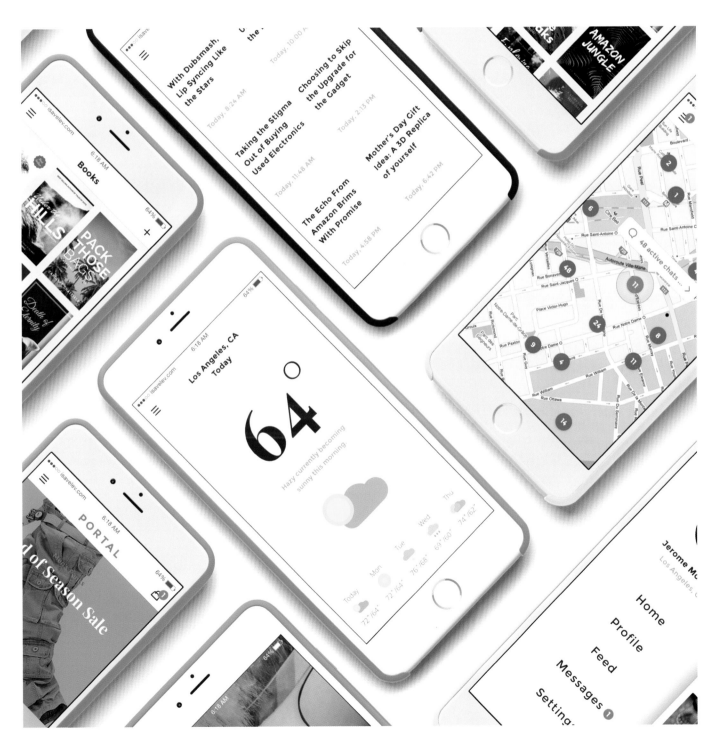

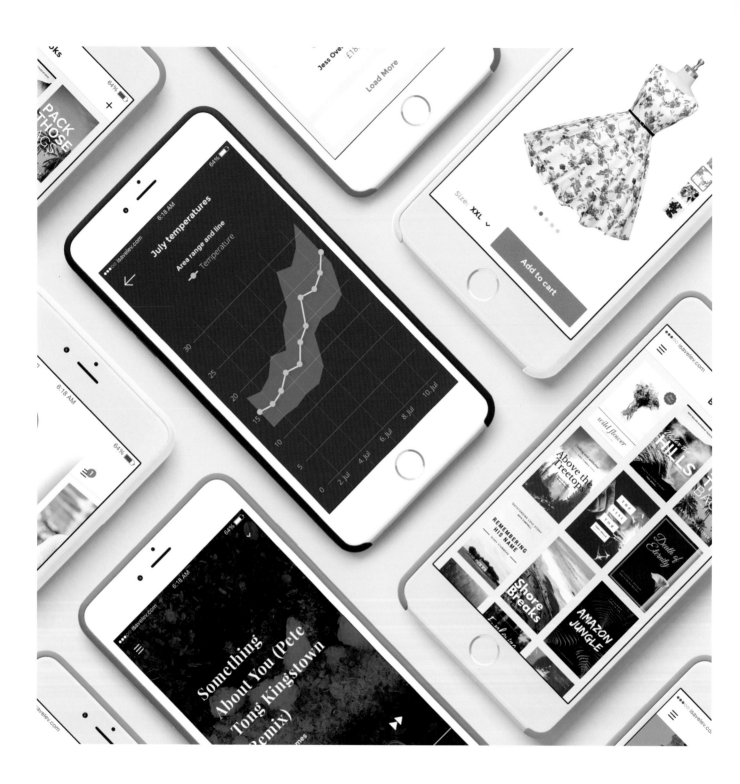

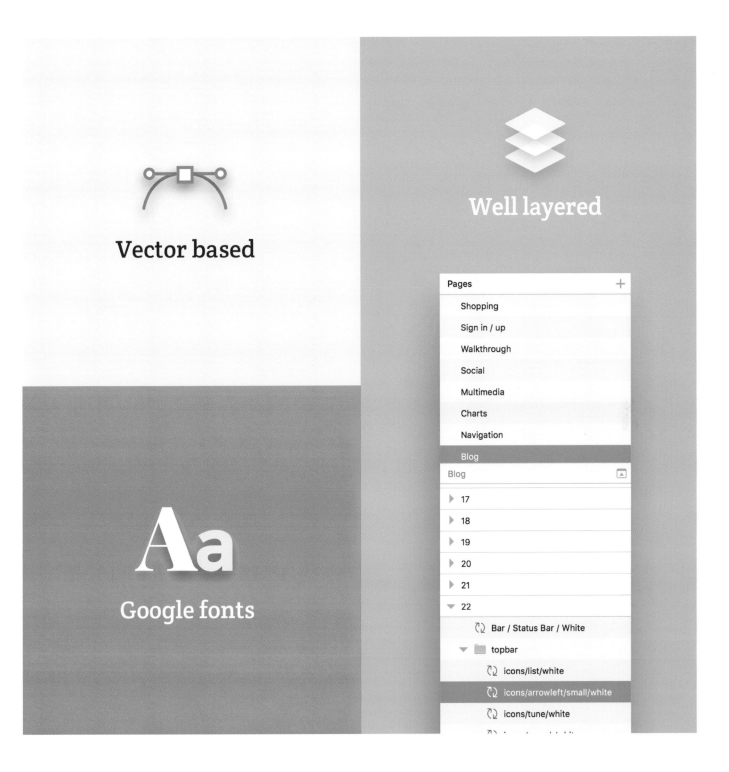

Vector based

Google fonts

Well layered

TOTUS

Designer: Igor Savelev

Totus is an on-demand app provider that help users get things fast and quickly. This app is an on-demand laundry delivery, kinda like Uber for laundry. It will start soon in Kuala Lumpur, Singapore and Hong Kong.

The city needs you more than you need the city.

Time is precious. No extra steps and nowhere else you have to go to drop off or pick up.

Totus is on-demand laundry delivery, kinda like uber for laundry.

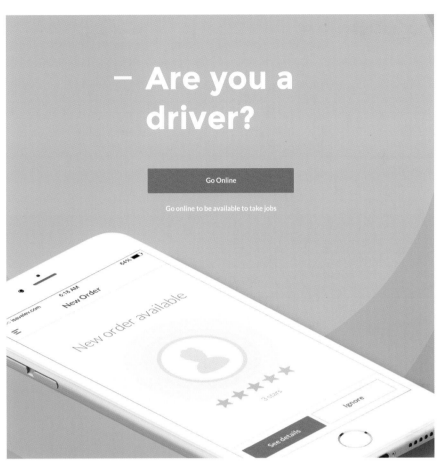

— Are you a driver?

Go Online

Go online to be available to take jobs

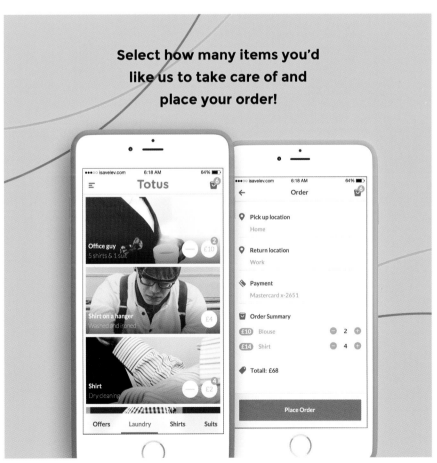

Select how many items you'd like us to take care of and place your order!

USABILITY AND USER EXPERIENCE IN INTERACTION DESIGN

Laszlo Svajer
Hungary

As a graphic designer, I try to make as strong connection as I can between the user and the theme. It's important from the beginning to find solutions that have emotional connections with the user. We should find the balance between the proven patterns (to be easy to use) and the new and playful solutions (to make new and interesting experiences). I like to use little twists to catch the user's attention.

I like to design innovative things, but it is important to use only where there is space for them. The usability is first. My most important tool is visual hierarchy. Every single detail, as the composition, the colors, the fonts and illustrations should support visual hierarchy. If the composition, the sizes and white spaces are well designed, then the user had a strong base to understand the interface and how it works. With the other tools (colors, typography, illustrations and pictures, etc.), I usually create mood and try to generate emotions. So the first is the message; the second is the concept; the third is the visual hierarchy and the fourth is the mood. It is hard to separate these processes because everything is connected with the others but this together should support the usability. Without one of them, the project is meaningless so I always check and recheck my work in every phase and I ask for an opinion from an outside person when I am not sure on something.

There are always new technologies like wearable devices, voice and movement recognition. In the near future, we will test them and they will fail or they will spread if they make more effective communication with the machines. The most important thing for me in addition to the effectiveness is the experience and joy of the user because we are not machines. The human factor, the emotions, should have an important slice of the future user interfaces.

INTERACTIVE RESTAURANT MENU

Designer: Laszlo Svajer

My example project is a restaurant concept and it is an interaction menu. I have collected the users' opinions on how they choose food. I have found four big groups: taste (especially spices), biological effect (the ingredients), emotional effect (desserts and the endorphins) and special experiences (foods from foreign countries, tradition and story). I've chosen four visual styles (which have connection to the four aspects) to show the message, and it needed a flexible umbrella identity to make it easy to use. The final product looks like a magazine because the guests use it like a printed magazine when they are waiting for their orders. They can browse pictures, information from the dishes (ingredients, origin, story, etc.).

In this menu there is always a big picture to illustrate the current food and there is a connection between the used graphic style (transparent ingredients to demonstrate what exactly are in the dishes, mysterious lights to make an unknown feel, surrealistic illustrations to show the tastes) and the aspect of that quarter. The user interface is in the same layout but in a different style to adapt the current quarter. The typography is very flexible. I painted 170 characters with foods. There is a possibility to select from different character styles (like ingredients) to create the mood which has connection with the current page. The titles are always unique in this way but they have a visual connection also to create a common identity.

Using this digital form of the menu is good for the restaurant because in this way it is easy to measure and control the orders. The dishes are easy to change (Maybe there are no more tomatoes in the kitchen and the staff can 'switch off' the dishes which contain tomatoes). They can offer seasonal dishes and drinks that fit well with the selected foods to offer a better and more complete service to the guests.

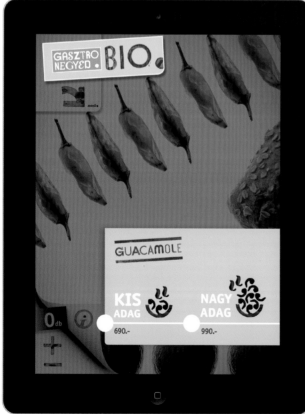

SKOLKOVO MAP

Design: Radugadesign   Country: Russia

During the work in Radugadesign, the designers have produced an iPad application which tells about Skolkovo Science City. The current app consists of two parts: Maps and Panorama. The Panorama is for exploring the plan of the city with all of the buildings in real time. It works with virtual reality technology. It allows you to see images of future buildings from the roof of Hyper Cube, which is in the center of the Skolkovo. At the same time, the Maps mode is helpful for learning a variety of information about the buildings in the city, seeing the 3D models with daytime sunlight as well as in night lights, reading about architecture and seeing a gallery with plans, drafts, photos and models.

AVOKADO

Designer: Aloïs Castanino   Country: France

Avokado is a subscription service that delivers healthy fruits and vegetables to you every day.

RADICAL RED
#FE2D63

RAJAH ORANGE
#FF9C27

BRIGHT SUN YELLOW
#FFD324

JORDY BLUE
#6V4FED

PASTEL GREEN
#72E371

Rubik - Bold

[**Main headlines**

Rubik - Medium

[**Sub header**

Rubik - Regular

[Praesent id metus massa, ut blandit odio. Proin quis tortor at risus et justo dignissim congue. Donec congue lacinia tor lectus condimentum laoreet.

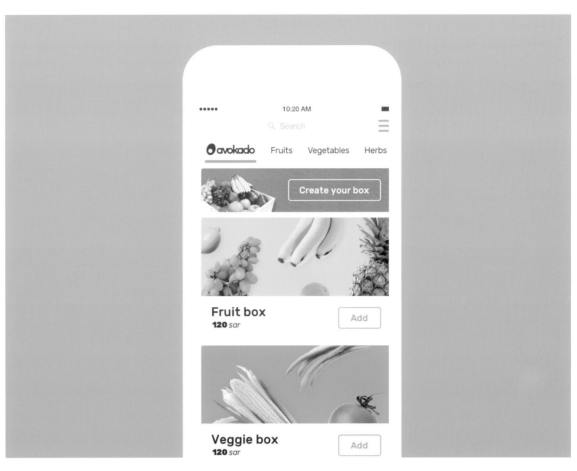

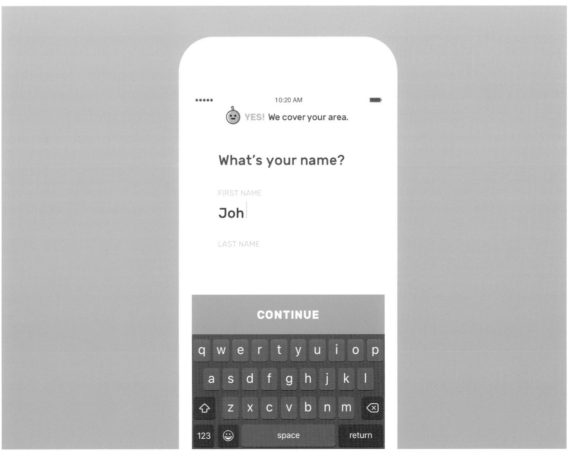

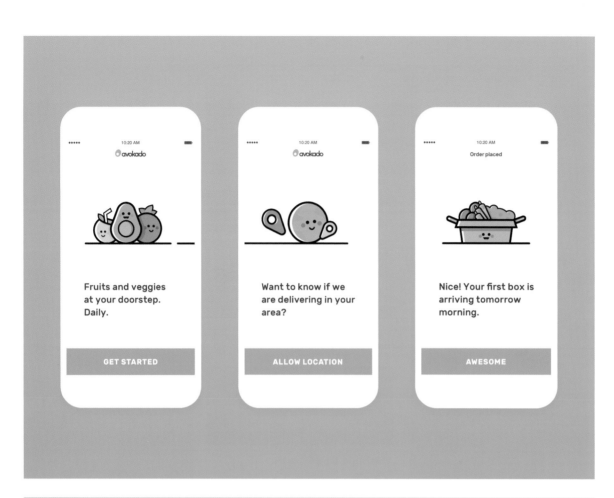

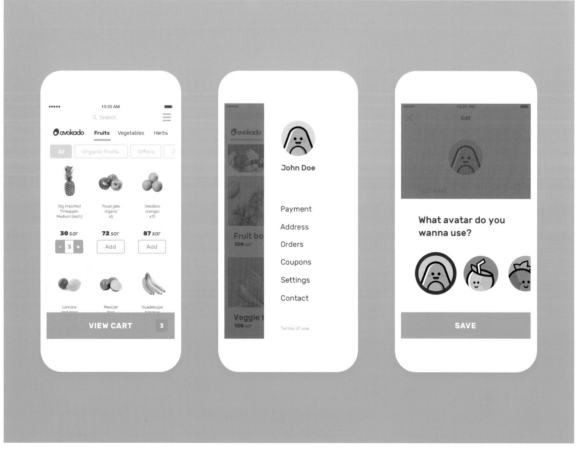

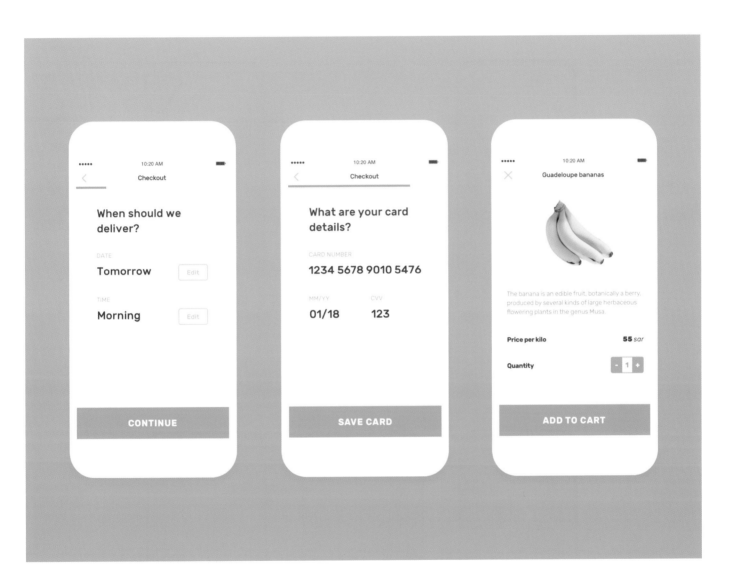

LITTLE SLEEPER

Designer: Alper Çakıcı   Country: Turkey

Little Sleeper is designed for babies and people who want to fall asleep easier. It lets you add your own recording, listen to ready-made sounds and loop sounds as long as you want.

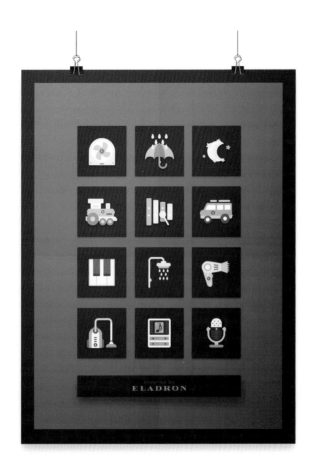

THE TRIAL OF FOOD-APP CONCEPT

Designer: Junliang He/Minyu Wu　　　Country: China

Modern food contains harmful additives and excessive nutrition, which consumers find difficult to perceive sometimes. Designers use traditional cultural elements in ancient Chinese trials and develop four main functions to analyze our food and give a conclusion. The app can serve as a guide for consumers when they are buying food.

扫描界面

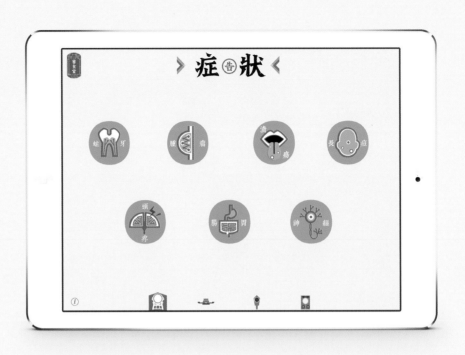

證人

點擊　查看

夜不能寐

元兇

咖啡因

限　半瓶

返

HEALTHCARE LIGHT

Designer：Mattia Becatti   Country：Switzerland

The aim of this project is the realization of a lighting system, consisting of different functions: Lighting, Training Mode, Chromotherapy and Wake-up Light. The system consists of an 80x50 cm panel, this dimension is in relation to the average dimension of the human body and can diffuse enough light without blinding. The system is provided with two dumbbells, which have the function of heartbeat sensors and are connected to the system. The system adapts the speed of the exercise representation to the user's heartbeat.

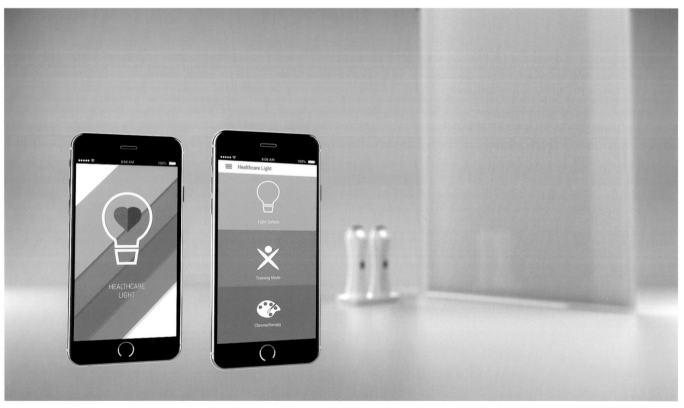

☰   Healthcare Light

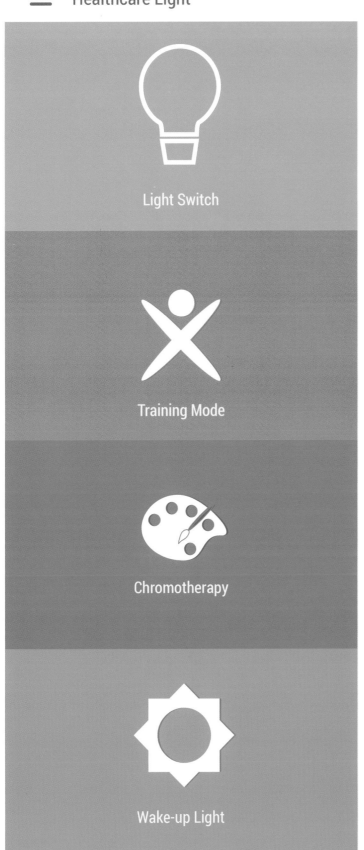

Light Switch

Training Mode

Chromotherapy

Wake-up Light

HEALTHCARE
LIGHT

HEALTHCARE
LIGHT

○ ● ●

A solution for everyone
to stimulate movement and visual
perception interact with light

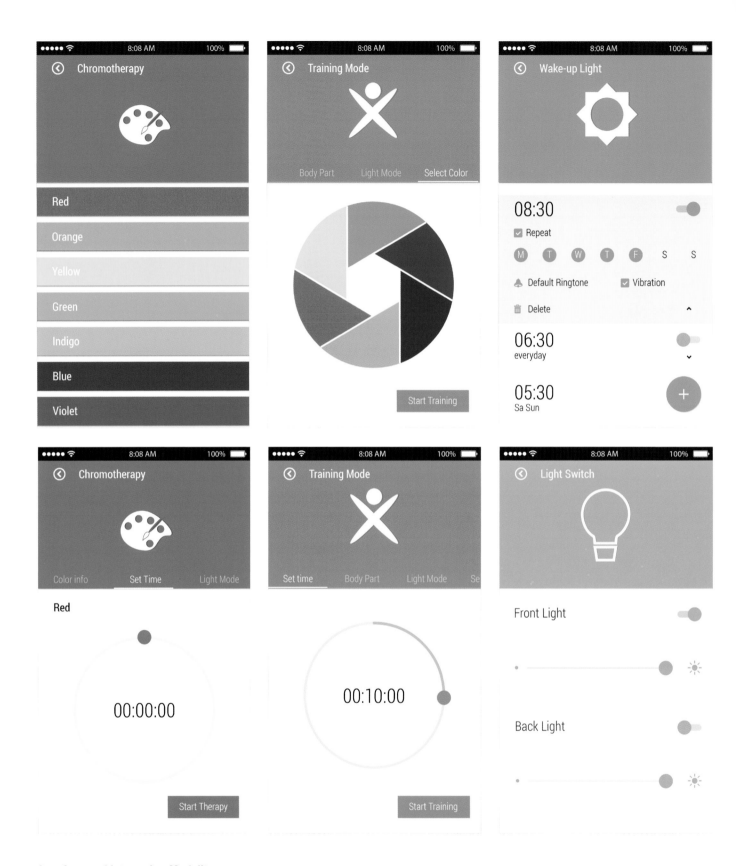

Interface and Interaction Modality

The main interactive feature is the Training mode, the idea to include a fitness function, using light as an element of representation. The panel is positioned on the wall. The wall has the function of surface. It is possible to project information, adding a new quality to the light. From the back of the panel, light beams are projected on the wall. The user has the task to follow the beam, using locomotor systems (arms and legs). The system of exercises helps the visual perception with coordination of movements by upper and lower limbs.

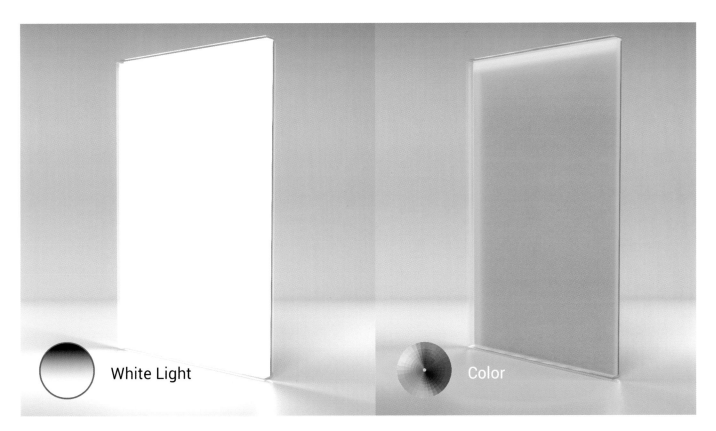

White Light

Color

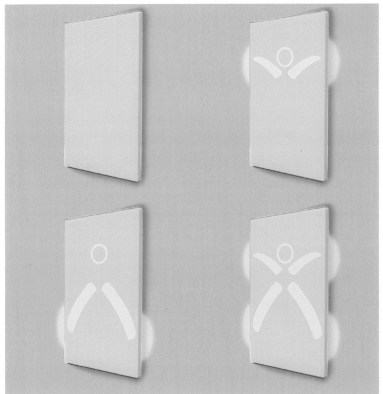

Research and Development Context

This system can be used for everyone, especially for senior people. As people age, vision is drastically reduced, perceptions of space worsens. This solution is good for them, because it is essential to encourage the relearning of the body's movement, especially in people with conditions of motor deficits, based on coordination between motor and cognitive activities.

User Experience

With this system the user interacts in a beneficial way for good health, both mental and physical, all as therapeutic system, by performing simple exercises which improve visual perception and coordination of movements or just meditating with the help of light and also greater wellbeing when waking up.

NOTES ON INTERACTION DESIGN

Frantisek Kusovsky
Czech Republic

The approach to my work is always same – design solving problems, not making things just nice, which is pretty person-specific anyway. Of course that does not mean it can't look good and also it does not mean design is only a visual layer. Design is everything. But a lot of people skip this and go crazy just making it "nice" which is nonsense and only attracts people with the same thinking, who will never help you to be better, because they look for the same, basic expectations. Please, do not fall into this trap.

Whenever I work on a project, I always think about who the users are, how and where they will use it. This is important. What devices will they use? In which environment? For what reason? Always ask as many questions as possible. It is important, otherwise you design for the wrong audience and the visual layer on top of your work will not save it.

Think of UI in the display on the typical airplane. How should one design that? In addition to the fact you have to have experience as a passenger on the plane (and if this experience applies on more aircrafts, which means more displays, it is even better for you). Now you have an idea about what you are going to design. But there are so many questions to ask before you can start. How is the display managed – via some devices or fully touchscreen? At which position is your hand touching the screen? Can it cover something important so certain navigation elements need to be placed in specific areas? Do all navigation elements make sense or should some actually be forgotten because they are not used at all (global volume option vs. volume option only when listening to something)? But it does not end only with interactions. In this case the devices are also important. What is the resolution? How easy it is to touch them, how they respond. How about the light conditions during the flight? There are a lot of questions to ask and answer.

Every (great) design is based on research, understanding, planning and exploration. In my app projects, I like "simplicity", but "simplicity" does not mean going crazy and making it unusable. Be sure people can navigate back and forth as they need. Be sure you do not hide important things and overall you do not hide various elements just because they do not fit visually. One of the approaches I try to apply to my work is a reusable design library. For example, in app design, I try to have certain elements repeating on all the pages, so they became major points of the app. And I am not talking only about navigation,

but some other, more or less subtle elements you can re-use. Based on that, one can build pretty heavy and complex UI design patterns while they still remain easy to learn and use for end users.

Try to learn the basics but also the ways to break them. Google Material Design or Apple Guidelines are great examples. Of course in many cases, knowing how and why to use them is crucial. They help you to understand various problems and solutions. But they are not chains. Do not stop there. Do not pack all your design solutions in one or another design pattern, style or trend. Think of *VSCO* – what a powerful photo app that is constantly challenging the UI, branding and overall design approach, while others follow the same patterns.

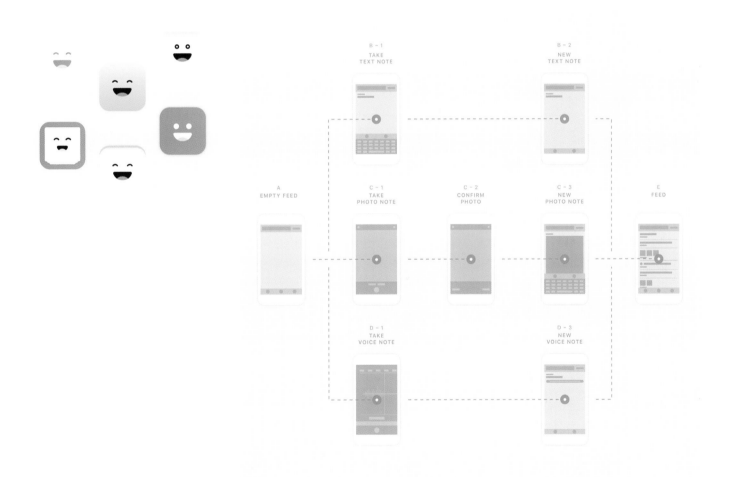

NOTTIT

Designer: Frantisek Kusovsky

Nottit App is a simple iOS app for note-taking. It was designed as a refresh and update to the default iOS app for note-taking. As an avid user of notes, the designer often needs to quickly capture his thoughts, whenever he is at school, in the subway or driving. The default app was not simple and quick enough. But Nottit app is a fresh approach to make it easy and fun to use. It combines refreshing, almost energized colors with simple icons, minimalistic UI that has good contrast and focus on the main elements.

Color palette

Sunrise

#e97e44 – #e98f44

Energy

#e97e44

Light

#e97e44

Fog

#e97e44

Dark

#e97e44

Typography

This is note name

San Francisco Text Light 32

abcdefghijklmnopqrstvwxyz

This is note date

San Francisco Text Light 24

0123456789

UI icons

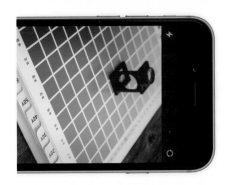

EASY NOTE

Designer: Iftikhar Shaikh   Country: India

Easy Note is a quick, simple and intuitive note-taking app which helps you to organize your life, keep all your information in one place, access notes even when offline and sync across all devices.

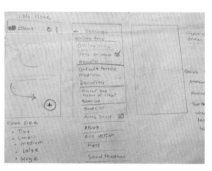

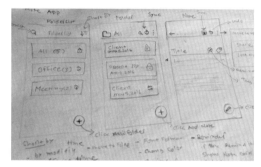

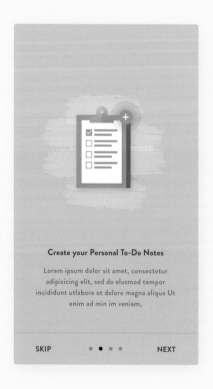

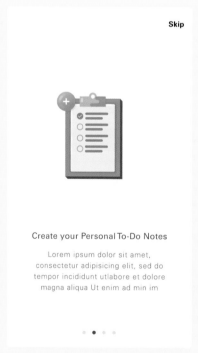

Create your Personal To-Do Notes

Lorem ipsum dolor sit amet, consectetur adipisicing elit, sed do eiusmod tempor incidunt utlabore et dolore magna aliqua Ut enim ad min im veniam,

SKIP   ● ● ● ●   NEXT

Skip

Create your Personal To-Do Notes

Lorem ipsum dolor sit amet, consectetur adipisicing elit, sed do tempor incidunt utlabore et dolore magna aliqua Ut enim ad min im

● ● ● ●

Create your Personal To-Do Notes

Lorem ipsum dolor sit amet, consectetur adipisicing elit, sed do eiusmod tempor incidunt utlabore et dolore magna aliqua. Ut enim ad min im veniam,

SKIP   ● ● ● ●   ›

Screen 1

▼ ◢ ▪ 22:20

Office   C ⋮

There is no note available
Tap on "+" to add new note

Screen 2

▼ ◢ ▪ 22:20

Office   C ⋮

There is no note available
Tap on "+" to add new note

Screen 3

▼ ◢ ▪ 22:20

All   C ⋮

File not found

Lorem ipsum dolor sit amet, consectetur adipiscing elit, sed do eiusmod incididunt labore

Screen 4

▼ ◢ ▪ 22:20

All   C ⋮

To do
Mar 18, 2016 08:00PM
🔔 Mar 21, 2016 08:30PM

Project List
Apr 12, 2016 11:30PM

Client
Apr 13, 2016 11:00AM

Update Presentation
May 5, 2016 01:00PM

Screen 5

▼ ◢ ▪ 22:20

←   ↶ < ⋮

To do

Mar 18, 2016 08:00PM   Mar 21 🔔 🏷

☑ App design
☐ Client Meeting
☐ Buy Gift
☐ Dinner with Hurin

Screen 6

▼ ◢ ▪ 22:20

←   ↶ < ⋮

Update Presentation

May 15, 2016 01:00PM   🔔 🏷

B *I* U̲ T̶ ☑ ▸

Mobile app of buy Sneakers and sell shoes Lorem ipsum dolor sit amet, consectetur adipisicing elit, sed do elusmod tempor incididunt ut labore et dolore magna aliqua. Ut enim ad min im veniam, quis nostrud exerctation ullamco laboris nisi ut aliqulpex ea commodo consequat. Duis aute irure dolor in reprehenderit in v velit esse cillum dolore eu fugiat nulla pariatur. Excepteur sint occaecat cupidatat non proident, sunt in culpa qui officia deserunt mollit anim id est laborum,Perspiciatis unde omnis iste natus error voluptatem accusantium doloremque laudantium, totam rem aperiam, eaque ipsa quae ab illo invenore veritatis et quasi architecto beatae vitae dicta sunt explicabo.

SEOUL IN MY HAND: OPEN FINANCE IN SEOUL

Designer: Kyung-hun Lim   Country: South Korea

The designer created this project for Seoul Metropolitan Government. It is a mobile web service that immediately reveals Seoul tax revenue and expenditures. Users can view annual revenue and expenditure charts by week, month and year.

Open finance in Seoul - SEOUL IN MY HAND

This project is a mobile web service commissioned by Seoul Metropolitan Government.
This service immediately reveals seoul tax revenue and expenditure.

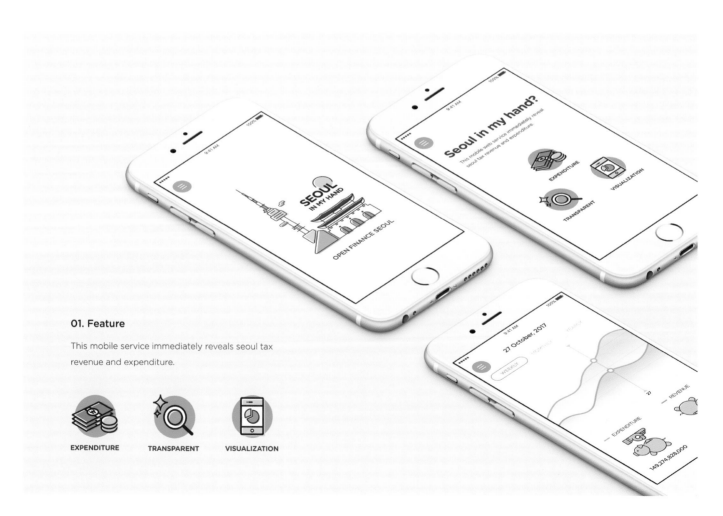

01. Feature

This mobile service immediately reveals seoul tax revenue and expenditure.

EXPENDITURE   TRANSPARENT   VISUALIZATION

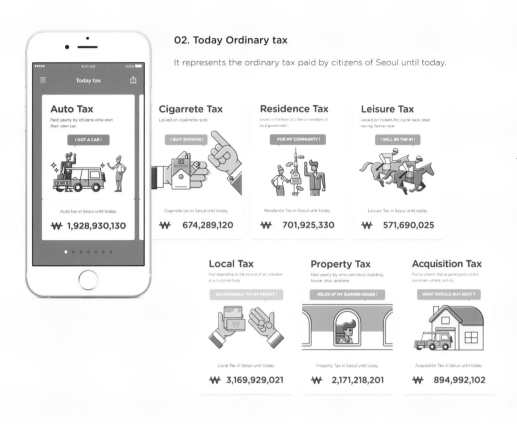

02. Today Ordinary tax

It represents the ordinary tax paid by citizens of Seoul until today.

Auto Tax
Paid yearly by citizens who own their own car.

I GOT A CAR !

Auto tax in Seoul until today.

₩ 1,928,930,130

Cigarrete Tax
Levied on cigarretes sold.

I QUIT SMOKING !

Cigarrete tax in Seoul until today.

₩ 674,289,120

Residence Tax
Levied in the form of a fee on members of local government.

FOR MY COMMUNITY !

Residence Tax in Seoul until today.

₩ 701,925,330

Leisure Tax
Levied on tickets for cycle race, boat racing, horse race

I WILL BE THE #1 !

Leisure Tax in Seoul until today.

₩ 571,690,025

Local Tax
Paid depending on the income of an individual or a corporate body.

ACCORDINGLY TO MY PROFIT !

Local Tax in Seoul until today.

₩ 3,169,929,021

Property Tax
Paid yearly by who own land, building, house, ship, airplane

RELEX AT MY SUMMER HOUSE !

Property Tax in Seoul until today.

₩ 2,171,218,201

Acquisition Tax
Paid by citizens that acquired products like real estate, vehicle, and etc.

WHAT SHOULD BUY NEXT ?

Acquisition Tax in Seoul until today.

₩ 894,992,102

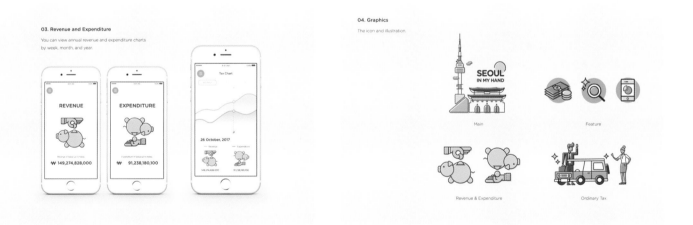

03. Revenue and Expenditure

You can view annual revenue and expenditure charts by week, month, and year.

REVENUE

Revenue of Seoul up to today.

₩ 149,274,828,000

EXPENDITURE

Expenditure of Seoul up to today.

₩ 91,238,180,100

Tax Chart

26 October, 2017

04. Graphics

The icon and illustration.

SEOUL
IN MY HAND

Main

Feature

Revenue & Expenditure

Ordinary Tax

ICOOK

Designer: Nitin Jain   Country: India

Icook is a food app which provides food shopping assistance. The app allows users to scan food items to search, save food recipes, gain information, and use their shopping list to find food items and buy them. It helps the user to order food easily and quickly without leaving home.

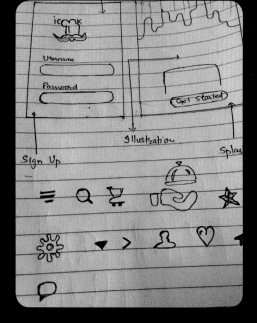

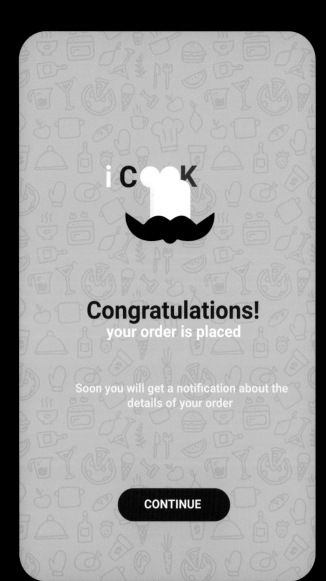

Profile

< **Profile** ⚙

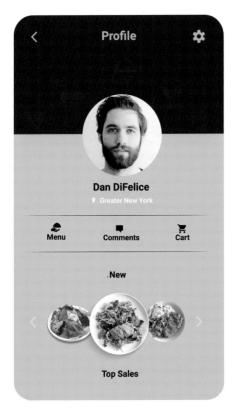

Dan DiFelice
📍 Greater New York

🤚 **Menu**   💬 **Comments**   🛒 **Cart**

New

< 🍽 🥗 🍲 >

Top Sales

Comments

< **Comments** ⚙

⭐

● ○ ○ ○ ○

Grilled Chicken
⭐⭐⭐⭐⭐ **4/6**

Dan DiFelice — 3 hrs
Tasty Chicken. I am very happy,
Thanks :)

Peter Kelvin — 9 hrs
Awesome food. We ordered a set
of it for the party tonight

Jumby kok — 1 day
Thanks for this , love it.

Leave a comment

[➤]

Menu

☰ **Menu** 🔍 🛒

Vegetarian

Non Vegetarian

Drinks

My Cart

☰ **My Cart** 🍽

Mixed Veg
450 g
$ 9
⊖ 1 ⊕

Grilled Chicken
500 g
$ 7
⊖ 2 ⊕

Cabbage Meal
500 g
$ 7
⊖ 1 ⊕

Subtotal $ 30
Shipping $ 5

Total $ 35

[**CHECKOUT**]   [**KEEP SHOPPING**]

Mixed Veg

< **Mixed Veg** ☰

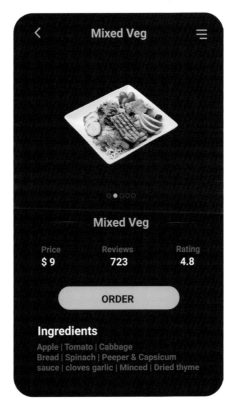

● ○ ○ ○ ○

Mixed Veg

Price   Reviews   Rating
$ 9   **723**   **4.8**

[**ORDER**]

Ingredients

Apple | Tomato | Cabbage
Bread | Spinach | Peeper & Capsicum
sauce | cloves garlic | Minced | Dried thyme

🔍 🛒

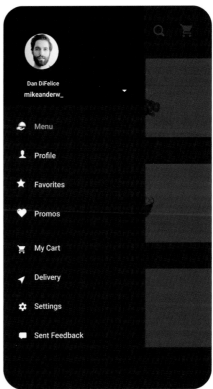

Dan DiFelice
mikeanderw_ ▼

🤚 Menu
👤 Profile
⭐ Favorites
❤ Promos
🛒 My Cart
➤ Delivery
⚙ Settings
💬 Sent Feedback

THE FUTURE OF UI

Ee Venn Soh
Malaysia

I believe in the future design will be and has to be inclusive. It has to be able to extend to a diverse range of users across products, services, environments or experiences. With the rise of voice user interface and technologies like AR/VR, we need to rethink how users are going to interact with our products. It is hard to keep up with technologies and trends but regardless of that, there is one thing that will remain the same, which is the user, the human being. The user should be at the center of all our design processes. There is no difference when it comes to designing for screens, services or anything else. Understanding the user, knowing the context of use, and ensuring our products are both useful and usable are essential. **As a designer, you have to be responsible for every single little design decision that you make.** It is even more true when you are designing for a large-scale product that has direct impact across millions of users. Your decisions will either raise or lower the barrier for people to use your products. It is hard to predict or say what the future will be like for UI given that the medium of interaction will be different in the future. How a person consumes information today might

be different in the future. But what we could do now is ensure that our designs have longevity, enough to survive through a period of time. We need to design future-proof UI. This can be difficult if you are the primary point person for the product design standards and guidelines.

You need to ensure consistency, scalability, modernity of elements and patterns. Stress test your design across different contexts and situations to determine what pattern is appropriate and what is not. To multiply the complexity, you need to consider more broadly how your design system will work across different channels and how it will synchronize across different teams. When it comes to shipping a product, instead of shipping a product with a complete total overhaul, you should take all the design vision and goals and break them into smaller pieces that you can ship, learn and iterate. It is a baby step each time. With data science and analytics, they can help you to see how it is working. You will be able to assess the public reaction or feedback and iterate from there.

GRAB

Designer: Ee Venn Soh

Grab is an online transportation network and technology company that offers a wide range of ride-sharing and logistics services through its app in Southeast Asia, specifically in Malaysia, Singapore, Thailand, Vietnam, Indonesia and the Philippines. The designer was asked to design a blue sky transportation app for Grab as part of a conceptual assignment.

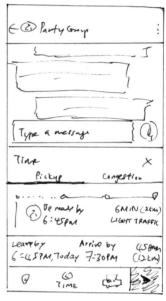

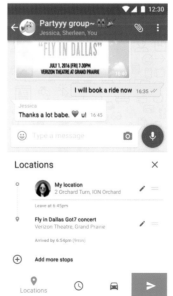

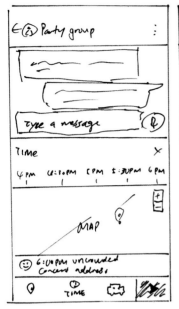
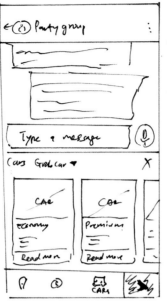

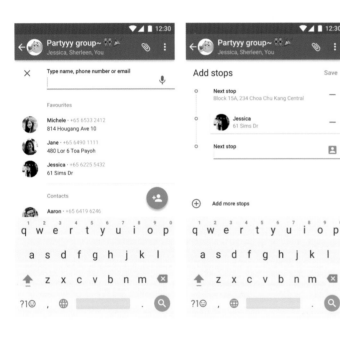
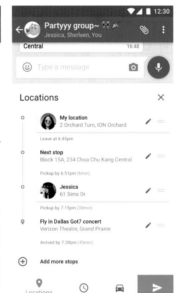
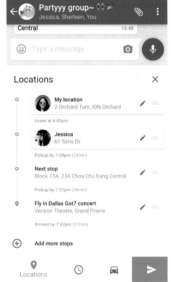

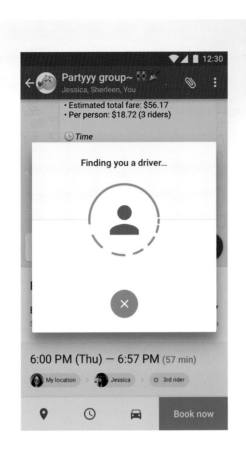

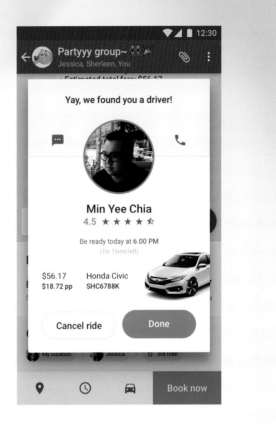

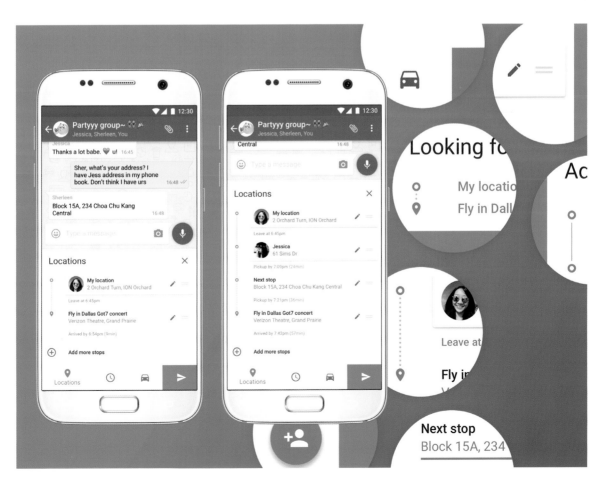

JETSTAR – RESPONSIVE ONLINE CHECK-IN

Designer: Ee Venn Soh

Jetstar currently offers a standalone mobile and a standalone desktop check-in service. Mobile has been built on a mobile web platform, while desktop is on SkySales (old monolithic platform). The designs, in particular on the desktop version, are out of date, and do not offer a consistent user experience. In addition, a large volume of our customer complaints received involve issues and confusion around the check-in process.

Jetstar have identified that they need to move the check in logic over to DotRez (responsive platform) from SkySales (old monolithic platform), and as part of this project the check-in experience should be redesigned and redeveloped to build a singular responsive website.

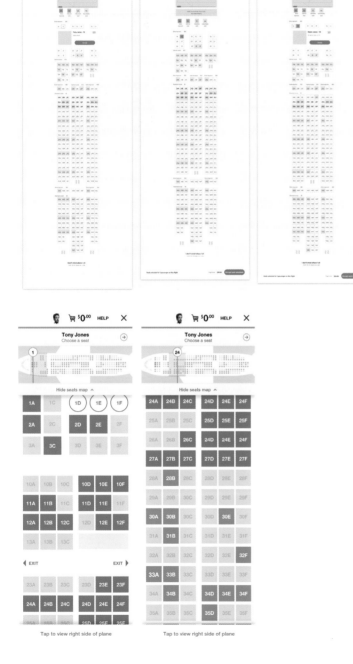

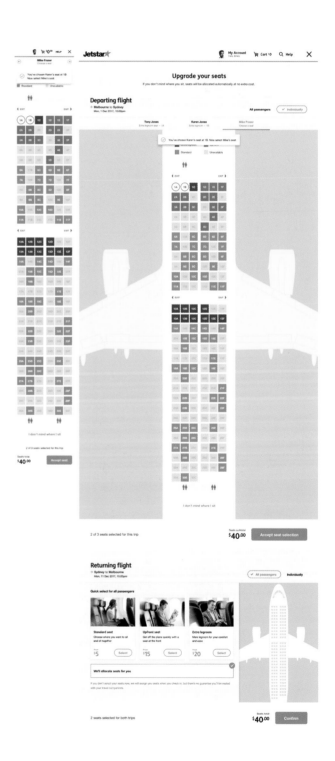

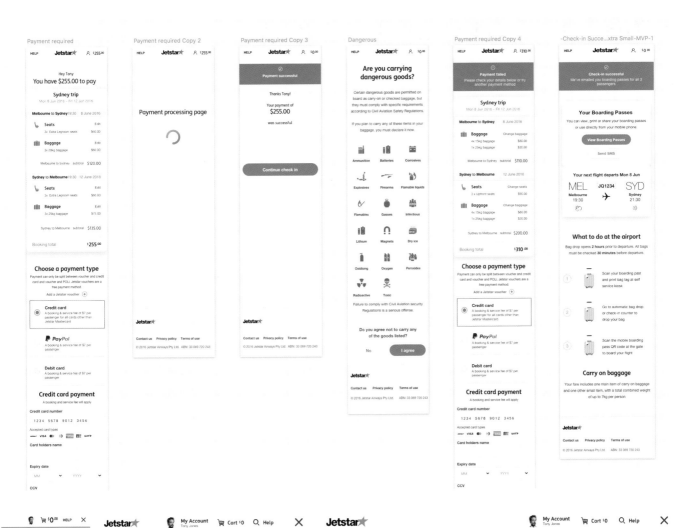

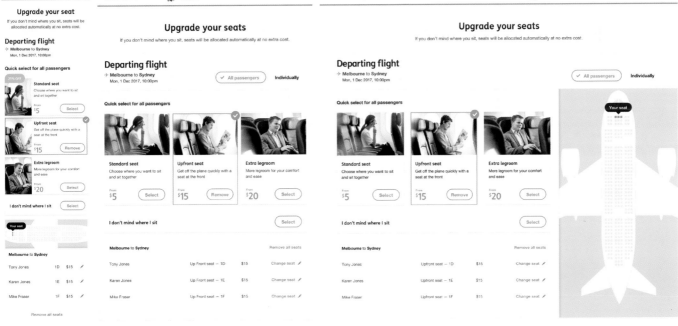

Mobile Phone   *iPad*   *Website*

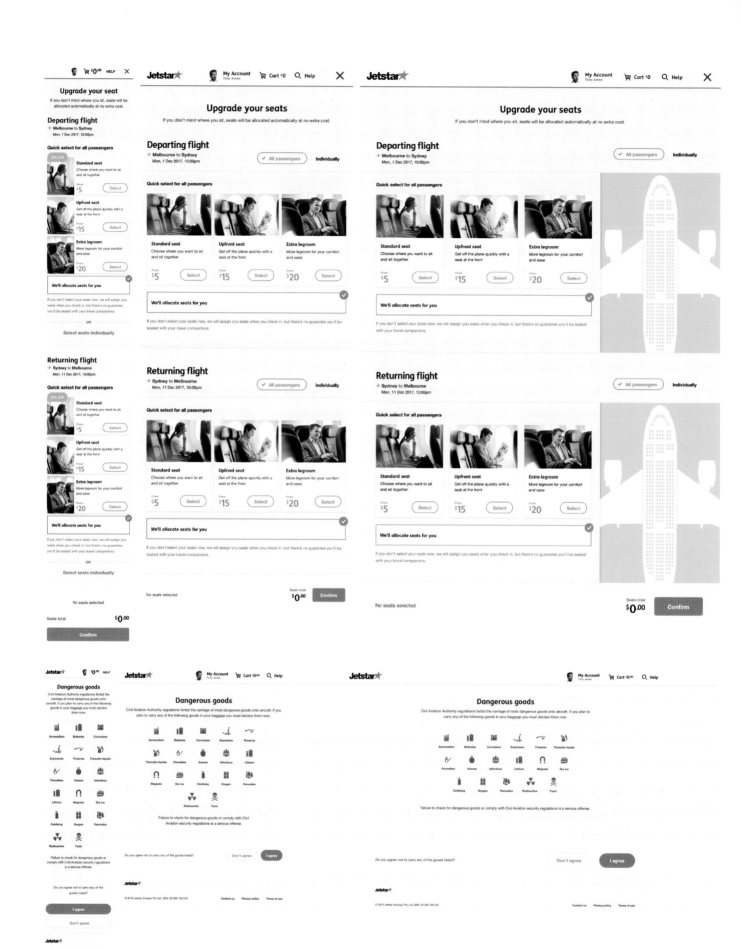

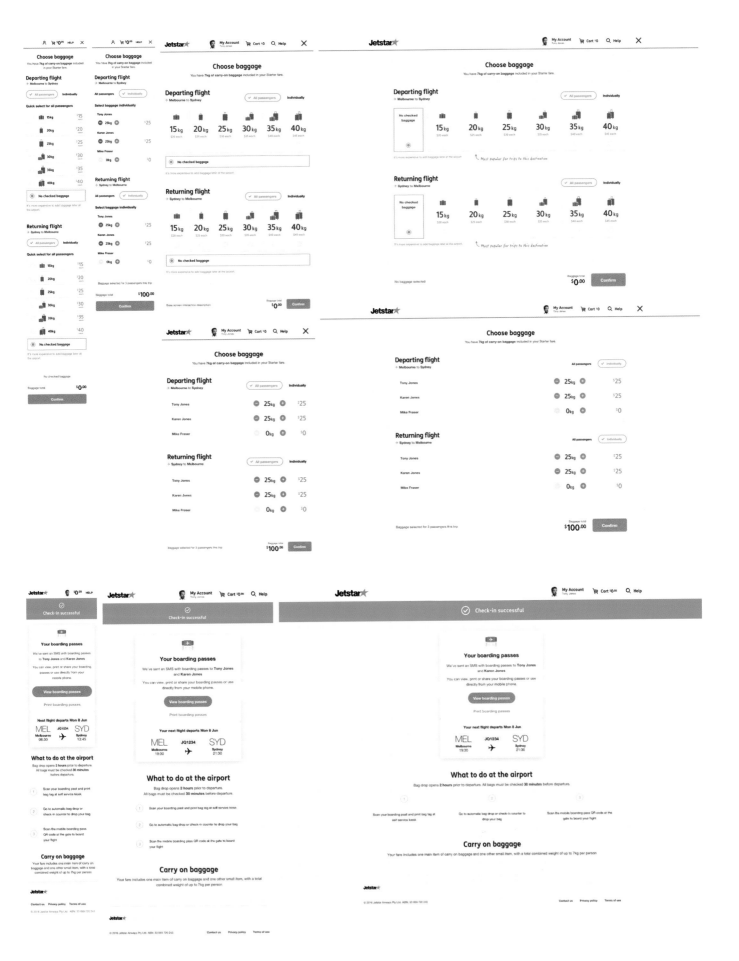

UFFIZI MUSEUM-APP CONCEPT

Designer: Saverio Rescigno   Country:Italy

Uffizi app will allow you to discover Uffizi Museum in a multi-sensorial experience. The use is very simple: you have to install the app on your Android or Apple phone, create an account and start to enjoy it. You have simply to frame the item and our guide will tell you everything about it, the author and the story. This use mode is the way for blind people. If you are deaf, you can read explanations on your screen.

SCHOOL PAYMENT APP

Designer: Mohammad Afzal   Country: India

This is a school payment app. There are two types of user, namely, Parent/Student & School. Parent/Student can create accounts and pay fees to school for any commodity student purchase, tuition fee, etc. School provides a registration function. Users can add school details and bank details, so that the same school can be selected by the student to pay fees.

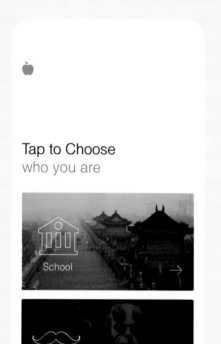

Tap to Choose
who you are

School

Parent

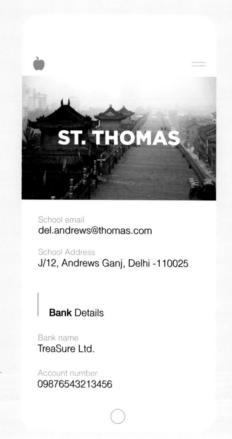

ST. THOMAS

School email
del.andrews@thomas.com

School Address
J/12, Andrews Ganj, Delhi -110025

Bank Details

Bank name
TreaSure Ltd.

Account number
09876543213456

Sleek

Bold

SURVEY APP

Designer: Mohammad Afzal   Country: India

The app was created to perform surveys in the city. Surveyor gets the details of the area based on login ID. Surveyors visit the survey location and verify the members at that address through the app and then lock the details/data.

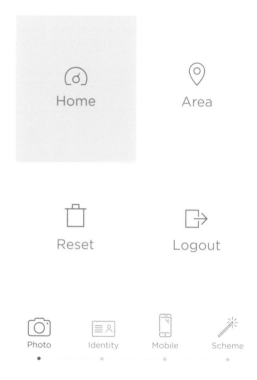

Lansdowne, Jolan

442 **4** **391** **2**
Members Surveyed Yet to Survey Unde

Name in English	Aman Bhoye
Father's Name	Ishwar Bhoye
	• Locked

Name in English	Aman Bhoye
Father's Name	Ishwar Bhoye
	• Locked

Name in English	Aman Bhoye
Father's Name	Ishwar Bhoye
	• Locked

Name in English	Aman Bhoye
Father's Name	Ishwar Bhoye
	• Locked

Verification

Aman Kol   • • •

Photo   Identity   Mobile   Scheme

Verification

Aman Kol

Saved   →

Verification

Aman Kol   • • •

Identity number
0256324120

Name as in ID

Validate by QR Code   >

Saved   →

INDEX

ACKNOWLEDGEMENTS

We would like to thank all the designers and contributors who have been involved in the production of this book; their contributions have been indispensable to its creation. We would also like to express our gratitude to all the producers for their invaluable opinions and assistance throughout this project. And to the many others whose names are not credited but have made helpful suggestions, we thank you for your continuous support.

FUTURE PARTNERSHIPS

If you wish to participate in SendPoints' future projects and publications, please send your website or portfolio to editor01@sendpoints.cn.